HEAVEN ON EARTH
IS A MISSION

by

BESS S. PERMUT

Also published by Bess S. Permut
"How To Find Your Way Back Home"

PESHA PUBLISHING

P.O. Box 47484

Phoenix, AZ 85068-7484

Printed in the United States of America

Library of Congress Number 87-92255

"Heaven on Earth Is a Mission" is the first book in the series of "Living on the Pathway to Heaven," copyrighted under #Txu 763-243.

DEDICATION

I dedicate this book to my beloved husband, Maurice, who has encouraged me to fulfill my mission on earth, no matter the cost to him. It has been his dedication and lack of selfishness which has allowed me the time to bring this book to fruition.

I am also dedicating this book to my dear friend and student of God's *Laws*, Steve Mangold, for without his encouragement, dedication, assistance with the typing of this manuscript, and his personal quest for *Truth* all these many years, I feel this book might never have become a reality.

It is said God sends to us that which we need when we need it. This certainly has been borne out in the appearance of Kim and Sam Roper into my life. It has been through their combined efforts–Kim's ability on the computer and Sam's encouragement, faith, and struggle to live—that has led to the culmination of this book.

To all who have helped along the way, I offer my thanks and love.

ANGELGRAPHS

Marcie Taylor, a kindergarten teacher who lives on a farm near Girard, KS, with husband Mark and two sons, took the angelgraphs on the front and back covers of this book. On July 10, 1997, as she was looking out the west window of her living room, she saw her angel in the clouds. She grabbed her camera and ran outside. She took two pictures using a zoom lens and one showing the relationship of the angel to trees in the foreground. Her 11-year-old son, Matthew, also saw the angel from his grandparents farm down the road. Marcie says the angel hovered in the sky for about 20 minutes. Oh yes! The camera has not worked since

TABLE OF CONTENTS
INDEX

Page

Page

Page

Page

Page

Page

Page

LIVING ON THE PATHWAY TO HEAVEN

FOREWARD
SECTION I

Dear Reader:

This is a story of a woman who as a very young child would play with her imaginary friends alone in the fields, the woods, and under her favorite chinaberry tree. She would be told of many magical things to come and how her life would be dedicated in the service to the Father and His children. She little understood what they were talking about at the time but the thoughts remained with her until the present day.

She grew up having to work most of her life in order to help maintain a home for her mother and two siblings, having lost her father at an early age. While working, she also put herself through college. After college, she married and served at Pearl Harbor during World War II.

She was to witness the awful results of the disaster of the bombing of Pearl Harbor. On that fateful day, she was standing by the window to see what all of the commotion was about and when she saw the damage that occurred, she started screaming at the top of her voice. It was as though she felt someone slap her face and say, "*Why are you standing here. Go and help. These are your brothers and sisters.*"

This was the most profound and significant event in her life. Then, as if in a state of emergency, her circle of once imaginary friends came to her aid; and in so doing, helped her learn what her purpose was on Earth.

It all started like a dream or a vision. It was as though she felt she was alone down on the Earth. She felt lonely and depressed. Then suddenly, it seemed she could actually see her thoughts as they seemed to tumble out of her mind before her and she could sense that she was not alone. She began to see women, all kinds of women, around her. The impression that was impressed into her mind at that moment was that the world around her was as needy and lonely as she felt; and that in truth, all had come to the Earth to help each other through their short lives on Earth. Though all were different, they were alike in that they all needed help to *Find Their Way Back Home.*

Suddenly the sound of a voice so full of love and joy reminded her that centuries ago men had been taught the dogma of *Truths to Live By*, but they had disregarded them and now the supreme price for their ignorance is illness, pestilence, and the like.

She was directed to help man overcome illness of body and soul by teaching him *Truth Everlasting*. The voice continued, *"Now you can see how long man has needed help; therefore, there is no reason why you cannot continue working on your mission on Earth for you are to publish books to help all of mankind. Now always remember that downcast eyes leads to destruction of this Earth just as you see the destruction around you now. Only enlightenment can save the land upon which you now exist."*

Having lived many years beyond those tragic times, she has been all that time receiving lessons from her Guides, Masters, and Teachers. The messages concerned events which were to occur in the future. She was also given advice for those people who would come to her seeking help about their lives. Her work helping God's children with her gifts has been constant over the years. At the urging of her Masters, she published her first book, *How to Find Your Way Back Home*, in 1984. This now is the continuation of the original work which she had been told in 1941 that she would be doing.

First, let us explain that there is nothing new under the sun. There are no startling new explanations of *Truth*. *Truth* is *Truth*. It is constant, never changing, ever simplistic, ever eternal, and everlasting.

SECTION II

We are all wondering what life is about and why we are here. How do we find our purpose in life? How do we find fulfillment? And, how do we find the faith to live day by day? Just how do we find our way in this great cosmos and how do I fit into the grand scheme?

This book will take you on a journey of discovery from the time before your birth to life after death . . . and help you live with all the confusion found in between these two realities.

The author has received many messages of *Truth Everlasting* from sources of *Light* and *Love* and has been instructed to share these *Truths* with all in the hope that some readers will find that same source of *Love* and *Light* so that they, too, can find their own answers to the questions posed above so that they may continue to move "onward and upward" on their journey back home.

Lessons of *Truth Everlasting* found herein are presented just as they were received from the Masters and Guides with as little editorializing as possible for clarification.

The reader will note that the author is being addressed on many occasions on a first-person basis and will be presented here as such--again to help the reader better understand the content.

The grammar may appear archaic as it has been transcribed exactly as received and the author has been instructed to present this material as dictated.

SECTION III

QUESTIONS AND ANSWERS

Q: How can man prepare for life everlasting?

A: Man must first ask himself why he chose to be reborn at this time and to live another lifetime. Thus learning the answer to this would cause man to do his best to fulfill his original covenant so that he could finish in one lifetime and not have to return time and time again. It would appear man had not learned to accomplish all that he has promised to do (the covenant we promised to fulfill before birth) otherwise this lifetime would not be necessary. There are some exceptions to this rule, i.e. some come back to teach their fellowman how to progress on the pathway that eventually leads us all back home or to our highest consciousness. These men and women have a choice to either go on to higher levels of fulfillment or to return to help others. Thus they too grow to a higher state of consciousness.

In the very beginning when the Lord appeared before us, He advised us in this manner: *"Gain wisdom on the earth, share it with your fellowman and equate this wisdom with lessons on life everlasting."* Thus it would appear man must learn or recall all the *Laws* or lessons he had originally been taught in order to be prepared for the next phase of living.

Q: *How many times do men have to live down on the earth?*

A: As I mentioned before, man can return as many times as he petitions to return if he can show how he can fulfill his mission that was left incomplete.

Now while I am on the subject of petitioning--I would like to explain a bit more as to how all of this is done. First, man does not seem to understand nor does he want to admit that he has chosen his life. But first man writes the whole saga of his life before it is reviewed by his immediate Teachers and Guides who surround him and who try to guide and direct him under certain guidelines. Then the hierarchy must review this outline before the Father reviews it. If they all agree that the time is correct and that the family he has chosen to come to can help him fulfill his mission, he is given permission to reincarnate. The procedure may even take centuries or it can be done in a few years; it depends upon how well the saga is written or then corrected with the help of the Teachers. Thus you see they make sure the mission can be fulfilled. My child, a mission can be fulfilled in one lifetime, that is all the time that man truly needs to live on earth before returning home to live forever with the Father.

Q: *You mean all of us have chosen our present lives?*

A: Yes, there are those Master Teachers or God's angels who choose to return to earth at certain times of their own volition in order to help man. Many of us are touched by these beautiful people and our lives are enhanced by them. It was by their choice alone that they appear among us. In answer to your question: Yes, man finds that hard to believe that he chose this life because in many instances he suffers, struggles and cannot understand why he would choose such heartache. He has forgotten his past lives that are recorded or computed within his mind or he would remember that which he had left undone. Many times we mistreat people in a lifetime and when we return to earth, we in turn are mistreated. That is why God tells us over and over, "*Love one another--love your neighbor as yourself, etc. Live the Laws.*"

Q: Do we always come back the same sex, religion and nationality?

A: No, man has belonged to many tribes and has understood many faiths, but they all go back to the Ten Commandments as a basis. God originally placed man on earth in tribes and told him to remain always together. We have disobeyed him in many ways.

As this saga is written by us, the sex is determined as to which will be most advantageous in fulfilling that lifetime.

Q: If we all had every life computed in our minds, why is it we do not remember them?

A: When a child is born, he or she goes through that period of forgetfulness and all the rest of our time on earth we continue to seek to learn our mission. When a child looks at the ceiling of the room and smiles and gestures, many parents think the child has gas. That is utter nonsense. The children are communicating with the spirits of the loved ones they have left behind when they reincarnated. Many children have unseen friends that they play with, that they try to tell their parents about only to be ridiculed by being told, "There's no one there. I can't see them, so there can't be such a person." Soon the child, wanting to please the parent, loses his or her ability to converse and visit with spiritual friends and loved ones. We take that ability away from our children at a very early age and it is very sad.

Have you never met a person you felt you've known before? Have you never met someone you instantly liked and wanted to encourage the friendship? Have you met someone that you immediately disliked or felt uncomfortable in their presence? Why would this happen? The soul of man reaches out to the soul of another with whom he or she had an intimate or positive relationship. The negative feelings come because the soul also recognized an unpleasant relationship or environment.

Q: *What is meant by tithing?*

A: We are glad you asked us the question. Men interpret this as meaning setting aside 10% of their earnings for a cause. It may be a religious order, a charity, or for those who are in need, etc. The greatest gift given by tithing is overlooked and that is 1/10th of your time and energy given for a worthy cause.

Is it not true that all you can truly give that is yours is of yourself? Man can easily write a check or give cash that he has put aside. The actual given time can be done in a minute or two and can be so impersonal; but when you tithe your time, you are involved with another human being--a one-on-one experience which allows you to have an exchange of energy with a person.

In earlier times a barter system was successfully used-- no money ever changed hands, but respect and love for a fellowman was not measured by any set standard like tithing.

Q: *Why don't I feel any warmth from my fellowman? Why can't I find love in my life? Why am I alone?*

A: In order to receive warmth or love from our fellowman, we must first give to them what we are asking for. If we do not understand what the word love means, we are not capable of giving and thus are unable to feel any compassion given to us. We often have given to us in abundance that which we continue to strive for without realizing the gifts we seek are already within our grasp.

To use an example as an explanation of what we are speaking: If a man is eating a beautiful peach and he says to a fellow companion, "This is the most delicious peach I have ever eaten," but the companion has never eaten a peach, how can he feel or understand what the peach must taste like. The same thing can be said of love and compassion. If we have never experienced it in our lives, how then can we offer it to others: We then allow that gift to escape our grasp when it is sincerely offered to us.

PREFACE

One does not just sit down one day and declare he or she is going to write a book without some purpose or reason for doing so.

> *This book came about after a miraculous healing took place. How many times have you read or heard about someone being miraculously healed? I must admit before this actually happened to me I was a bit skeptical, but after September 11, 1984, I became a true believer.*

While on vacation in September, I became very ill with a fever of unknown origin. We were visiting Lake Tahoe, Nevada, and the doctor there could not ascertain the cause of the illness. After four days of lying in bed, I instructed my husband to pack the car that we were leaving for home early the next morning--no matter how ill I felt. Somehow I sensed I would die if we remained there any longer.

We drove fifteen hours straight to get home. After arriving there, my doctor was also puzzled at the cause of the fever. He took blood samples for testing. The results were shocking: No white blood cells! He began to tell me that I was a very sick woman. The blood tests indicated that I had no white blood cells to fight the infection. Each day for one week he drew blood, only to have the lab send back the same negative results regardless of the doses of the medicine he had prescribed.

When my condition worsened, he sent me to a hematologist who immediately informed both my husband and me that I had a fifty-fifty chance of surviving. He increased the dosage of the same medication and had us return early the next morning for a bone-marrow test to learn if removing my spleen would help. The hematologist also was at a total loss to explain the cause of the illness or the cure.

That night--as during the previous night--I could not sleep. I would doze off for a few minutes only to awaken with terrible pain. Then suddenly at 2:00 a.m., I awakened to see a halo of white light over my entire body and suddenly the sweetest, kindest and most consoling voice spoke. "Take the four pillows on your bed and stack them up behind you; now sit up against them. No, turn a little more to the left." Suddenly the pain lessened and a calmness settled over me—something I had not felt for ten days.

Then the voice continued,

"This is not your time to come over. You have much more to do to teach people about life everlasting. You must get that manuscript completed without any further delay. Since you are a Master Teacher, your students will ask you how such an illness could happen to you and now we are going to give you the answer: "There is an interim period in every man's life. If you had accomplished all that you had been commissioned to do, you would return now, but first all of the manuscript must be completed.

"We want you to know that this illness did not come from God. Nothing negative comes from Him--only love--only the greatest love man can imagine. There is always an outpouring of His love greater than you can imagine. All of the negativity and the evil that is on the earth comes from man himself. Do not judge any man, for only God can judge since only He knows the pathway each of us has chosen so as to fulfill our covenant. God loves all of mankind equally. All men are His children-- there are no special ones. What kind of a Father would He be if He showed partiality to one over another as earthly parents

sometimes do?"

Then I was asked to look up and it looked as though someone had shot a Roman candle or huge sparkler into the sky. I began to look at all of these particles of light and then the voice said: *"Watch the light; bring it into yourself for that is God's light and God's gift to you and you know that God's light heals everything."*

I then reached up to pull the light into my chest where I had the most pain.

Suddenly I heard the voice say: *"This afternoon at ten minutes of 2:00 p.m., your doctor will call and say, 'Mrs. Permut, you have created a miracle! Your blood has turned completely around in 24 hours!'"*

When the phone rang that afternoon at the designated hour, I was afraid to pick it up for fear it would not be the doctor and that I had dreamed the whole episode. (Oh, we of little faith.) But true to my kindly angel, the doctor repeated the exact words that were spoken to me at 2:00 a.m.

Then I remembered the voice warning me: *"You must take it easy for a couple of weeks until we are able to help you rebuild your energy level. Then after that you will be good as new."*

These identical directions and warnings were repeated by my doctor on the phone!

In two weeks I had gone back to teaching my metaphysical class and in six weeks the manuscript was put into book form. It was only then that I finally experienced a great peace that came over me. As the days went by, I began to understand that each day is truly a blessing and a new beginning. I began to see life differently; my priorities had changed.   This experience taught me what my beloved angels had been telling me for years: *"We can truly enjoy heaven on earth."*

What was unique about my visitations was that my husband was a witness to the light. He had been sleeping in a room adjacent to mine so I could rest more comfortably. When I needed his help, I would turn on my bedside lamp and almost miraculously he would appear. He had been awakened by the spiritual light and when he walked into my room he noticed the lamp was not on, but that a tremendous white light hovered over my entire body. He backed out of the room so as not to disturb what was taking place. He sat watching the clock in his room for ten minutes; then the light faded away.   He was hesitant to return to my bedside as he knew I was either being healed or being taken away. When he reached my bedside, to his amazement I was sleeping on my back in a deep, peaceful sleep. I had not been able to sleep on my back for over a year due to an injury and there I was, sleeping like a baby.

At 6:00 a.m., I awakened and turned on the light. He immediately appeared as though he'd been sleeping with one eye open. He helped me up and I started to tell him about the strange happenings. Before I could continue, he asked me one question: "Did your vision or your dream have anything to do with a huge, white light hovering over you?"

Since that visitation, my back is healed, no more fever, etc. It is true. "God's light heals everything."

If I had had any doubts before my healing about there being a living God and the relationship between man and God, it certainly was eradicated at that time. Believe me, there is a living God and He lives within each of us. He loves and cares about each of us equally. It doesn't matter who or what we are.

The voice informed me that my mission on earth would not be complete without teaching mankind about *Truth Everlasting and Life Everlasting,* that the so-called truths that were being taught were not true. Much has been lost in translation from one language to another.

They also alluded that some of the subject matter being taught on earth today is taught in order to control mankind. Teachers deliberately changed God's words even though when God had given them originally, He had felt they were being etched in stone and were to be taught forever. Now He sees these greedy teachers embellishing upon His truths in a negative way, frightening people by picturing Him as a vengeful God instead of the forgiving and benevolent Father that He truly is.

I had denied and fought my mission for many years making excuses for not writing His truths as He had explained them to us so many, many times over the centuries. Somehow mankind refuses to fulfill his or her mission even after they are aware of what they are to do.

After the healing, I knew I could no longer postpone this book. For those of you who read and study the words that have

been brought to me, it is possible they will help you find your mission. When you do get on the pathway, you are truly enriching your life because you lose all sense of fear. Thus, a peace and harmony within occurs and you will sense a new beginning in your life, then realize that each day is truly a new beginning and a blessing.

As you study these pages that have been dictated to me by my Master Teacher, you learn how fear can ruin your life. You give up entire control of your life when you feel fear. You give up your connection with God. As an example, you fear for your safety. He cannot come into your mindset when your mind is filled with fear. It causes Him to lose His ability to communicate with you down on the earth. As an example: If your phone is being used and your best friend wants to call you with an urgent message, how can she communicate with you? So to keep the lines of communication open with God, rid your mind of fear. Put your entire life into God's hands.

As you read further, you will learn more about what we learned from one lifetime to another and how some lives teach us lessons from the kindergarten to the 6th grade. Using that information in the next lifetime hopefully we can go from the 6th through the 12th grade and then on to the college education that represents the next life or *"Life everlasting."*

Having said that, I am reminded that the voice repeated over and over again that the Lord loves all of mankind equally. *"Remember,"* He said, *"It matters not to the Father the color of the skin, the creed he has chosen to follow nor his sex. He loves them all. Would that His children loved Him with such compassion and divine respect.*

"We have told you that this is your interim time. Had you finished your mission, we could have taken you back home. Each man has purpose for living on earth. Remember that the divine purpose of life is to learn what one's purpose is while residing among the living. Once you have learned your mission, you must reach out to help others learn about theirs. That is one of the Father's Laws. This is one explanation of the commandment, Love Ye One Another."

PART I

IN THE BEGINNING

FREE WILL

This incident which we are about to relate to you left an indelible memory in our memory bank. We found ourselves gathered together on a mountain when we suddenly heard an explosion of sorts--a big boom--and we found ourselves propelled to the very top of the mountain. We felt alone and dejected, not knowing where we were and why we were here until, at long last, we heard a voice harken unto us within our mind's eye: *"You are here to demonstrate to all of man that mankind can live alone on top of a mountain far away from the Father."*

That was the beginning of reality. We felt completely alone and helpless--helpless to the plight that had befallen us. Why were we here? Why had we been chosen to demonstrate His theory of evolution on this mountain? The more we thought about it, the more dejected and alone we felt.

We again heard His reassuring voice telling us the reason as to why we had been sent away from Him:

*"Regardless of how you might feel," He said, "we have to demonstrate once and for all that you have minds of your own. I have given you free will. So now, I beseech you to use it. Prove to Me that you can find your way safely back to Me. All you have to do is use and demonstrate the Laws I have constantly taught you. I have sent you My headmaster as a teacher. He will continue to re-educate you until you understand the meaning of **Truth Everlasting**. Until you learn all the lessons exactly as I originally taught them to you, you will have to continue to live on the Earth."*

We knew no man among us remembered all of the lessons exactly as we had been taught. We lamented that fact to Him. We had used our free will--not really listening attentively when He taught us--and had thus set ourselves apart from Him and His lessons until it finally dawned upon us what the true meaning of *Truth Everlasting* really meant. It started with our basic responsibilities toward one another. Had He not explained to us over and over again in the beginning that we were to care for one another, love one another, that another's problem automatically became all of our problems? All of us were responsible to seek answers as how to alleviate another's hurt. These were the basic parts of our daily lives and laws, thus part of *"Truth Everlasting."*

He continuously advised us, saying:

"Cultivate the land, till the land and it will produce food for you; and above all, use your minds." He reminded us, "Please do not forget the lessons My Masters and I have taught you. You must educate your mind each day, listen to your Teachers, and amaze yourself with the knowledge that you can learn through using your mind wisely."

We felt the Father had set us aside, so to speak, and even worse had deserted us when He went on His way back home. It disturbed us no end to see Him leave for we feared He had left us forever.

Another happening frightened us since we knew not of thunder or lightening. Suddenly, the Earth shook; lightening struck out in many directions! Each of us thought we would never forget the emotion we felt at that moment until the end of our times. Was it happenstance or was it reality? We finally figured it out later when we were given another example of His cunning ways for there suddenly appeared out of a cloud of dust another man exactly like us! It continued to happen until many men stood before us. They were men like ourselves. It seemed they were waiting for us to speak to them for they did not move until we advanced toward them. Their thoughts were as ours exactly as the Father had taught us. We knew then the Father had sent these men to teach us how to live among men.

We began to converse together through our mind's eye and we were surprised to learn they understood exactly what we had been thinking. One remembered part of a *Truth*, another remembered another part, and so we were reconstructing the *Lessons of Truth* that we had been taught.

So you see, my children, that was the beginning of men coming together so they could learn how to live together. The Father had sent these men to teach us how to live with each other, to understand their ideas, so we could better comprehend our own. He wanted us to live together to prove to Him men could live together on the Earth without fighting and arguing just to prove their own point of view. Men can articulate and reason their differences, thus coming to an agreement of thoughts, but today they do not sit down at a table for discussion as they could. Rather, they fight it out on a battlefield.

Then one day out of the blue, the Father appeared again, saying: *"Help each other, learn from each other, and continue to communicate together. For each of you has in his mind the evolution of Truth, each knows it all or some part of the Truths that I have been teaching all of you. Now stay together; accumulate enough energy to be able to return safely home to Me."* Without further ado, He left as quickly as He had appeared and until this day none of us has been able to see His face again nor have we accumulated enough energy to be there beside Him on the very top of the mountain where we had prearranged to meet. Eventually, we had hoped that sometime or somehow we would be able to make sure all of us together would remember His *Truths.* For until all of mankind understands His *Original Truths*, we will not be accepted back on the high level we had enjoyed before the "Big Bang." We must continue to teach each other and look for the brighter day. For when we remember His *Truths*, He will acknowledge us forthwith.

THE LORD'S PROMISES

In the beginning when the Lord appeared before us, He said, *"Gain wisdom, My children, and equate wisdom with lessons on*

Life Everlasting." Yes, if you learn how to live in this lifetime, you will be rewarded in the hereafter. He sent us back to live alone on the Earth when He found how dependent we had become upon Him. He told us we could come to see Him when we were sad, when we were despondent, and when we were truly in need. *"I shall always be nearby."*

He had become aware that He had kept us from gaining energy because we no longer thought for ourselves; we had become dependent upon Him for everything. We felt completely at a loss unless we saw His light or heard His voice.

We often reminded Him of and echoed His promises to us, *"Come unto Me and let Me send you away happy."* He had told us this over and over again. Then He began to sense the uneasiness in which we lived because of where He had placed us. We were fearful that we would not be able to contact Him as readily as we had in the past. Again we felt fear and loneliness. He gathered us together. He explained that we were not learning how to depend upon ourselves or learning the lessons He wanted us to learn while living on Earth. He was, therefore, assigning the Hierarchy of Angels to come to us to help us direct our energies from this time forward. He told us we could call upon them and that we should not be afraid of life--that they would watch over us as closely as He had in the past.

"I must relinquish My hold on your lives and allow you free will to live and express yourselves in your own way, in your own definition of your life." He informed us that later on we would discuss our errors and our hopelessness. *"If you will only remember My teachings, they should guide you and should have taught you how to live according to My Laws."*

Since our learning was limited to His discussions with us, we felt we had lived in vain before He announced He was releasing us. Now we gathered together and sought recognition from every alert person and deep thinker. We wanted to master their understanding of the *Truths*, and also their understanding of what the Lord had taught. We amassed lots of energy in this fashion, and we too began to understand that in the past we had become too dependent upon the Father. When we began to communicate with each other, we learned to accentuate the positive ideas and we drove out the negativity from our minds. If one man insisted upon being negative, the rest of us tried to wrest his ideas from his mind, replacing them with our positive thoughts. We learned anew each morning how to stand up and say, "O Lord, Master over all mankind, we have attained ambition again. Thank You for setting us free. In doing so, You have helped us to become deeper thinkers and greater achievers on this Earth. Forgive us our transgressions from the past. Help us to learn how to live together as one big family. Please, O Father, let us assemble together again after we have mastered all of Your *Truths*."

My child, later on in this lifetime, men will have to assemble all these thoughts and prayers and somehow insert them--even if haphazardly--into mankind's minds. For until we are able to cause all men to grow, little will be attained by those who live on the Earth. Man must learn how to envision himself standing upon the mountain top, hearing those *Truths* being taught by the Lord over and over again. The greatest progress mankind has made since his rebirth is to understand these *Truths*:

- *Life exists after death*

- *Mankind beholds the mystery of life and death each time he views the birth of a child*

- *Each new birth brings all the knowledge and wisdom*

from past lifetimes, recorded within its own mind.

Mankind utilizes *Life Everlasting* through the process of birth. He only understands one part: That life is continuous and that he manifests *Truth Everlasting.* In other words, if you record *Truth* and it is accepted as being *Truth Everlasting* and if *Truth* continues to live, why then cannot man be considered as *Life Everlasting*? Because if *Truth* lives, so does mankind.

THE LORD'S MERCIES

In the beginning of time, the Father spoke only *Truths.* He had a tremendous amount of mercy for all of His children. He felt mercy in His heart for them because when He realized the inadequacies of man, He sought ways and solutions to impress upon His children the necessity of their learning and remembering His *Laws.* He tried to teach them that His *Laws of Truth* would always live and they could manifest them through positive thinking. If they had faith in the Father and His *Laws*, there would never be a need for fear. He instilled these thoughts into men's minds. He reminded man every morning upon awakening to not only greet him but to also actually visualize their lives as they wanted their lives to be.

The Father pleaded with them not to accept fear of need or want of any condition in their lives. But, unfortunately, man refused to listen.

Instant Gratification Can Leave Men Needy

Men cast about to find solutions in their own minds. They constantly reminded themselves of the inadequacies they felt. They did not want to refresh their memories every day with new ideas; they wanted only enough that would be adequate for the moment. In this way, they relinquished all of the new thoughts once taught them by the Father, thoughts which could have seen them through difficult times during their whole lifetime. Because they had deserted these *Truths*, of course, they did not have what they wanted. They began to blame the Father, feeling His thoughts were not enough. They felt revulsion; so they earnestly tried to forget all that the Father had taught them. They thought it was just too much for them to handle. It was too much effort to put forth. Later, they felt as much revulsion for themselves as with the Father. What they wanted in reality was instant gratification without having to work, without having to think, without having to remember, just as the youth of today wants everything right now or, better yet, yesterday. They think and live as though there will be no tomorrow. Then in moments of retrospect, they fear they have not garnered enough on which to live.

Men Choose to Turn Away From the Lord

Some even began to worship evil ones or idols instead of the Lord. When the Father saw what was occurring, He sent a Master Guide to them. Alas, they also repelled the Lord's Master Guide, saying, "We do not need His help anymore. We want to be able to live with our own thoughts that we find within our own minds, not the more 'Holier than thou' that we have been taught!" They proclaimed a holiday for themselves and set forth to conquer the world on their own terms.

The Masters, feeling their mission of *Truth* not able to be accomplished, returned to the Father and mankind was left alone to live in vain. Thus, today if man goes seeking for the Father in prayer or thought, he has a difficult time expressing what he sincerely feels. In turn, the Masters of *Truth* also have a hard time convincing themselves that man really wants to straighten out his life on Earth and earn his reward by conforming, listening to and learning the *Original Truths* because man has become so distant from the Lord.

Again, a new wave of thought is becoming fashionable, for mankind to listen to and learn. The perpetrators want to establish a new precedent among mankind. They proclaim themselves as prophets of the occult. They simulate discussions with the Lord and then try to convince others they are teaching the truth. If they are lucky enough to see the light around the Father's face, they immediately tell the world they have seen it all, that they have mastered it all, and the occult world is no longer a mystery to them. They send messages back and forth for others to hear and heed, but in reality they have established nothing. Few men have reached the state where they can prophesy for mankind. Many who alter their state of mind for just a moment will immediately think of himself as a prophet. This sends out false signals to man, and once again the newest fashionable precepts are found wanting. Each man can be his own prophet. All man has to do is salute the Lord every morning, asking for guidance and direction, and if he will allow himself the time for meditation, the answers will come.

Those few prophets who exist on the Earth hide in shame because of the pseudo-prophets and their hypocrisy. They also fear to reveal their true identity for fear that, if they spoke the truth, mankind would destroy them.

A reminder: When man prays, he is asking for direction and help. When he meditates, he is listening for answers.

THE BIRD'S SONG

The teacher continues: This was the first lesson taught about responsibility.

We are God's children and we know that God loves us all, but He knows just as parents know today unless children are taught to be responsible for their own actions, they cannot live the life of respectfulness for themselves or others. They stop loving themselves and have poor self-images and thus spiritual growth is lost and their missions unfulfilled.

Now to begin with this truthful story: All of mankind was taught these *Truths* in the same way, but we refused to listen. We would seek our haven of refuge in our minds and hide there, thus closing out His teachings completely. Eventually the Father understood what we were doing and decided to teach us a lesson. He thought that would cause us to realize how important it was to learn His *Laws*. It was not just to make our own lives more complete while we lived on Earth, but also in the *Hereafter*.

He sent us away from Him. We soon learned a hard lesson. Where things did not flow as easily as they had under the Father's guidance and where once we had lived peacefully and harmoniously, now things were disruptive and we began to feel animosity toward one another. It was then that we slowly came to the conclusion that we had indeed been very stupid in not listening and now we had to renew or review our minds hoping to find the needed words of *Truth* that we had been taught. We gathered around us every man from our village and asked them to please search their minds to help us reconstruct just one simple *Truth* that we had all known and had been taught by the Father. Soon even those whom we disliked among us helped put together one simple *Truth*. Suddenly the Father appeared saying:

> *"Thank you for trying to help yourselves. Now hunt for deeper thoughts among yourselves so that you can remember all of the Truths you need to know to find your*

way back home. They are truly simple thoughts."

We began to despair once again for it had taken all of us such a long time just to construct one *Law* that the very idea that we had wasted all the time we should have been learning these *Laws* made it even harder for us to endure. We felt we were totally lost from the Father. Suddenly, a bird flew over us singing his little heart out. We listened and listened intently; his tune commenced to make us feel light of heart. It had distracted us from our worries so we decided to try to emulate him. As we listened, words suddenly started to fit in with the tunes that he was teaching us. Then like magic, one by one, thoughts were formed. Eventually all of the lessons came together. We suddenly realized that the Lord had sent the bird to exist among us to teach us these *Truths* again.

After awhile the bird flew off; but as he was flying, he thought he heard a man groaning as though in pain down on the Earth. The bird decided to fly low and investigate, thinking perhaps he could be of help. Lo and behold, it was the Lord who was imitating a man in distress so as to attract the bird. He said to the bird:

"Thank you My fine fellow for you are indeed a Master Teacher among all of mankind. You were the first and only one that stimulated the men's minds and so the men understood what you meant by your songs that you sang. So I not only thank you for them, but I thank you for Myself. I bless you to continue to fly safely for you have braved the seas and the mountains to fly this distance to help your fellowman. I, your God, bless you and entreat you so that you may continue to follow your instincts and find other men so as to expose them to your songs. I shall continue to bless you throughout all eternity. You have won My admiration and respect forever. Adieu.

With this, the bird flew off knowing he had fulfilled his complete mission and has forever followed the Lord's orders and has helped countless men to survive even unto today.

FOLLOW YOUR LIGHT

(A Parable)

When the Lord first left us upon the Earth, He told each and every one to listen carefully to the following words: *"Follow your light and you will surely find Me at the end of your pathway, waiting eagerly and earnestly to receive you safely back home."*

As it happened, all but one young man understood the directions that had been given. This man had been slow in understanding any of the lessons of *Truth*, and none of his fellowmen had tried to explain them more clearly to him. Thus, this one man understood little as to how difficult it would be living alone; he did not understand as the others had that there was safety in numbers. All of the so-called wise men were ready to set out on their individual pathways regardless of whether their family or friends wanted to come along. They gave their families a choice, which was either to follow them, if they wished or not. They also explained that it was a gamble, but they had to follow the Lord's instructions and follow their light.

You see my child, here was the beginning of setting one's self apart from another, and the slow-thinking man stood his ground and decided he would stay behind. He felt the Lord would come back to the original place that He had placed them. For days he sat next to his family and waited to be retrieved. Slowly he began to understand, as the days grew shorter, that he had best try to find the other men. He had been pre-warned that as the days grew shorter, the winter or cold would be upon the Earth . . . and he was ill prepared to face that alone.

The Father appeared to him in a dream and asked him why

he still remained so far away from the others. *"Why didn't you follow My directions and follow your light?"* The man replied, "I was afraid of leaving You alone, Father. I thought You would come back here and discover that we had left and You would be alone." The Lord replied, *"My son, you did not follow My orders. I told you to follow your light, that I would find you wherever your light took you. So now take your family and follow the light that I leave for you."*

The man set out alone, without his family, saying to them, "Come along if you wish, but the Father has told me to follow my light." The Lord spoke out to him saying, *"No, again you misunderstand Me. I told you to take your family along to follow their light also."*

They began their long journey together. The longer it took, the more miserable the man became, for he was sure that he was lost and he became very frightened. Suddenly, one morning, after a long, exhausting night, he awoke to find himself near the wise men. These were the same men who left him behind. When they looked up and saw him, they were in total shock, wondering how he could have come along so fast. He greeted them and said, "The Lord, our blessed Father, left His light for me to follow you so that I could easily find your light. You see, the Lord wanted us to live together forever. He told me He could find us wherever we live."

Thus, once again they set out together; but this time the wise men taught the younger man all they knew about the lessons of Truth and lo and behold, he soon understood the meanings of the lessons more clearly than even the wise men had understood them! He explained to them the exact meaning of this lesson, of this story. One thing they certainly had to learn was not to set themselves up as judges of all mankind because only the Lord has the measurements of each man's mind. He and He alone can tell whether a man is true to His lessons of *Truth*.

It is not for a just, humble man to judge. Mankind still has to learn this lesson. They continue to set themselves apart from other men. They single out the ones they like and those they dislike. As long as this continues, there can never be peace and harmony on the Earth.

COMMANDMENTS

Good morning, my child. The Father explores all manner of ways to reason with us. This kindly Father defers judgment on us until we use our very last breath and then expire. The Father has sent His highest Angels to talk with us today. You have listened patiently for those words of wisdom to seep into your mind. We are not absent from you during your daily meditation. We allow you to join with us using His light on high. You manifest the thoughts of *Truth* that we are expounding upon today. If mankind will only allow himself to live on high, he will despair no more. If a man refuses to allow other men to insert negativity into his mind, he can climb to the highest of mountain tops as far as his growth in consciousness is measured.

The Father has allowed us to live on Earth for centuries, so to speak, hoping we would find the magical words of *Truth* that He had once taught us. Thus, when you read how the prophets sat down together to relate and compare their thoughts, they discovered the *Laws* which were originally taught to all of us, one by one:

1. *"Thou shalt not kill."*

2. *"Thou shalt not commit adultery. Thou shalt not covet another man's wife."*

Adultery was not considered at the very beginning of time. That was a latter day's usage when *"Thou shalt not covet thy neighbor's wife,"* was added. These were only a few *Laws* taught to us, then:

3. *"Thou shalt not believe in any other Lord than Me." These thoughts were placed in our minds each morning when we saluted the Father.*

4. *"Thou shalt not use profanity in My Name. Thou shalt only live on the high level."*

5. *"Thou shalt not live in vain." In referring to this, they added "Truth shall set thee free."*

6. *"Thou shalt not covet another's kid nor his heifer." Yes, we adored our cattle during that period of time, too, for were they not of God's creation?*

7. *"Thou shalt abstain from thinking evil thoughts." It allowed us to harken back to the Lord each morning so we might sit down together and relate the lessons of old.*

The prophet went on to say, "He sent back to us at that time exact quotes which He meant us to live by:"

8. *"Never envy another person nor relate a fabrication or lie."*

9. *"Thou shalt love thy fellowman and ease his burdens, for*

his burdens are your burdens and must be shared."

10. *"Thou shalt love thy Lord God with all thy heart and all thy soul, and thou shalt teach thy children and each man you meet the exact same Truths so that he, too, can teach his children."*

We take leave of you for today.

MAN REFUSED TO LISTEN

The Teacher awakened me about 4:00 A.M. to dictate the following lesson:

"We are trying to awaken within you and mankind the fact that at one time we were all able to sense the Father's nearness, His thoughts and His love. Today, even as we are speaking, we forget He is listening very carefully to each word that we say.

"According to tribal laws, which were sent down to us centuries ago, we understood only that He spoke into our minds. Each day He would bring to us a different lesson. Then several lessons later, He would search within our mind attempting to have us recall all the soft-spoken words that He had brought to us. The Father assumed that we had understood all of His lessons, but according to what He discovered while He was searching within our minds, He learned that we had sought refuge from His teachings and had substituted our own versions of what He had said to us."

Man's Distortion of God's Truths

This was the original distortion of His *Laws*. He tried to teach us over and over again, hoping each time the real *Laws* would remain within our minds. Those of us who had learned them diligently and understood His teachings would occasionally feel the impulse to say to Him, "Don't You see what is wrong, Father? You have spoiled us by spoon-feeding us every moment of the day. Now we are unable to retain what it is You have taught us."

The reality of the harm that we had brought unto ourselves did not occur to us until, finally, the day of reckoning occurred when suddenly we realized that we were not able to understand or retain the fountain of thoughts that He was bringing to us. They had all gone astray. When we realized this, we cautioned our minds not to accept His thoughts at all. When we recognized His thinking had supplied us with a daily ration of food for both mind and body, we suddenly understood how hard it was going to be to comply with His wishes if we no longer understood His thinking.

How on Earth could we feed our minds and bodies? Ravaged men and women began to understand the holocausts that had come down upon them. We all despaired, but He no longer appeared before us. Suddenly we felt alone, no longer able to harness the energy flow that He supplied each morning upon our awakening. We missed the Father's strategy and guidance, which He had hoped we would learn, so as to always remember and feel throughout eternity.

More than feeling alone and dejected, we realized that communication with Him was impossible for we had forgotten how to relate to Him because His *Laws* were no longer alive within our minds. We continued to salute the Lord each morning, but received no response from His side of the veil. Thus, men even today feel He is so far away. In *Truth He* is within us, but we have failed to accept that as a *Truth.*

We now begin to search for even one word of His original *Truths,* hoping that we again can account for each of His *Laws.* The Father too is searching for ways to help us so we can return home to Him. He is seeking solutions to aid us in avoiding the abyss or void created by us within our own minds. We now seek His company once again. We wish we could see His face and share His mind-set and thoughts once again in the hope that *Truth* would once again flourish within our hearts and minds.

Some of us seek a holocaust hoping to wipe us out of His mind entirely, and suddenly we understand why men choose to die without communicating with Him. Their ignorance caused them to fear His wrath, but the all-loving Father would welcome us home with open arms, no matter what our sins on Earth had been.

HOW JEALOUSY BEGAN

On this particular morning, as I sat down to type, my Teachers appeared eager to commence a new topic: *Truth Everlasting*. "This is the grandfather of all topics," they said. "Listen carefully to how man's responsibilities on Earth will be outlined. Much of man's destiny was pre-programmed before birth." This had never been alluded to during my years of contact with my Teachers so I tried to record word for word of that which was said.

We should adhere to our original thinking; we advocate no changes be made within the mind's bank. We should demand only the *Truth*, the *Absolute Truth*, as has been manifested by the Father's lessons. We are saying this to you because man comes pre-programmed to fulfill his destiny and should never allow any outside force to de-program his mind.

It is as if you had designed a blueprint for a new home that was to be your ideal home. You hired an architect to check it over. When he returned the print, he had taken such liberties in changing things about that you could hardly recognize your original plan. You are angry, but you have to begin recreating your original plan. This is what happens to man who allows his mind to be de-programmed. Life on Earth is too short to waste the time.

The Lord allows us to use His light. We must first agree on a topic for discussion. We must then discuss it at full length from all points of view like the subject of *Truth Everlasting*. That particular subject would take a Teacher almost a lifetime to teach a student the entire manuscript. So we are advised to teach it bit by bit so that man can acquire and absorb a piece of it from time to time. It is our hope that we can continue in this manner to advance more on this topic of *Truth Everlasting* as time goes along, until finally all of the *Original Truths* have been reproduced.

Mankind's Responsibilities

It is the responsibility of all of mankind to learn how to meditate deeply enough and become consciously evolved enough to understand the teachings that his Teachers try to inculcate into his mind. His responsibility does not end with his evolvement. It is only the beginning. His next responsibility is to share with all of mankind the exact *Truths* as taught by the Lord in the very beginning. When He taught us the *Original Truths*, He did not substitute one word for another. It was all pure *Truth* that had been imposed upon our minds. The Father accused us of not listening carefully enough. He would repeat the same subject over and over again until we digested it all fully. He wondered if the time would ever come when we would be able to teach all of this information to enlighten other of His children. Then He refrained from teaching us all of the lessons, but little by little He discussed different subjects with different peoples but never again taught all to all people. In other words, He discussed all of the subjects, but the most difficult ones were given to the most astute persons and the easier more logical ones were given to the less alert minds. Eventually, He had hoped the alert minds would teach those who were less alert. We had grown accustomed to hearing His thoughts from Him as He taught us and we began to resent the others with more alert minds trying to teach us the Father's lessons. So, stupidly, we decided among ourselves to half listen to their teachings instead of putting our minds to the real test of absorbing all we could learn. We turned a deaf ear to those more alert men. We then sought after the Father, wondering why He refused to teach us exactly alike.

The Beginning of Jealousy

The Father felt remorse for having assigned the tough subjects only to the alert minds. He felt remiss because He saw and felt the hurt that the less active minds felt and understood their attitude toward their fellowman. This was the beginning of jealousy. That is when the less active mind began to dislike the more active or intelligent man. Rather than subjugate themselves to learning what they could learn from whomever could teach them, they would allow their minds to accept only the teachings that came directly from the Father.

Thus until this very day at this very moment, many men still feel reluctant to learn from a person with a higher degree of intellect or education. Even though man is trying to help them to help themselves, trying to help them find their way safely back home, it is sad to observe that we have learned so little throughout the ages.

HOW THE LORD TAUGHT EACH OF US

From the beginning of time, the Father has come back into our lives to educate us. We have all stood together at one time or another during many lifetimes--but in the beginning we were very young souls who banded together in tribes. We stood before the Father each morning--this is after He placed us upon the Earth. He educated us with His *Original Truths* over and over again. He usually began by saying, *"Do not forget a word of what I am telling you. Let Me verbalize this in the same manner that I spoke to you yesterday."* He admonished that we should not allow another person to distract or revise His teachings. *"Set your minds free and understand each word that I am now teaching you""*

We were set free upon the Earth with free will, but He sent us a support system to help sustain our lives while we lived down on Earth. The *system* was that His Holy Ghost would stand before us each morning and would stand close enough for us to see Him. Thus, you must learn about the state of altered consciousness. Our imaginations ran away with us. We stood still and gazed at His figure before us, and then He said, "*Say not one word out of line; say it just like I have taught it to thee. Set your mind into motion to accept these thoughts like I have been teaching them to thee.*" Then He began again by saying, "*Clear out the recesses of your mind now and repeat unto Me the exact words I have spoken unto thee.*"

He discussed with us our mistakes, but seldom did He rant or rave at us. The Father used a definite term of endearment so that we could understand that He loved us regardless of how many mistakes we made. He altered our state of consciousness in some manner so that a direct terminal went into action until we finally understood every word that He had taught us. He always set the time as to how and when another lesson would be forthcoming. Soon, He used His divine manner of thinking so that He would bring each thought through to fruition and then allowed us a moment to concentrate upon the subject. Then He would ask us our opinion of His thoughts. Soon a discussion occurred, but He seldom imposed His will upon us. Later on in these discussions, He would say to us:

> *"The ghostly apparition, which I am at this moment, will soon disappear. As you each stand before your fellow men, you must learn to abide with them and live closer with them than even with yourself; and above all, spread the words of knowledge which I have thus instilled into your minds."*

He seldom repeated His stance, but once upon a time He taught us all the *Original Truths*, and thus rewarded us by reminding us how to remember them. One by one He placed them into different categories. He used a number system: Place this one in a One position; place this one in a Two position; this one in a Three position, and so on, until he reached the Eleven position, and there He stopped. He had placed those numbers in a sequence only He understood. Father used them simultaneously in such a fashion as to illustrate how they fit together. They ran one into the other, and into the next, until following His directions, they all made sense for us. He used us as guinea pigs, so to speak, helping to refine His material and define His position so it would be easier to teach the next group of recruits who He was going to place down on the Earth exactly as He had placed us there.

Now to understand how hard the Lord worked with us, you must understand it was a daily ritual for us to amass enough energy to stand beside Him and use His brain--so to speak. We understood His exact words, in the order of the day, and soon we had memorized every word of His truthful display of knowledge and *Laws*. By investigating and searching our minds He soon understood how difficult it would be for us to remember all of His *Laws*, so He placed one *Law* into one person's mind, another into another's mind, and then into even another group in the hopes that someday we would all get together and piece all the puzzle together until His lessons became so ingrained within us we could not forget.

The Father understood the difficulties that we would face alone, without His help. So, He brings His Holy Ghost to us each morning. We can then ask for advice from Him and the illumination that He brings to our brain helps us to understand

His responses.

My dear child, this lesson has more meaning than meets the eye. We do not want to continue with this further today, but we promise to return and inculcate more of this same type of energy into your mind so that you will understand how man began to think and how the original thoughts were placed into his mind, for it was all telepathic then since no one spoke. When he learned how to use his mind, man learned he had a great power within his mind; and that if he could learn how to correctly use it, he could overcome every obstacle that might be placed in front of him while he resided on the Earth.

This is a mistake mankind makes today; he is so fearful of living life that he forgets to be objective and to accept and to understand God's teachings. He relies upon himself completely and allows fear to overshadow everything that he faces. This makes life much more complex and certainly incomplete. God promised us that if we remembered and studied and lived by His *Laws*, extending our knowledge unto all mankind, He would help make our lives simple. He would fill our lives with happiness and joy; and when we returned to the other side of the veil, we could truthfully say that we had lived in "Heaven on Earth."

And so, bless all of mankind who comes within the radius of your smile. It costs nothing to smile and give of your love. That was the first expression that the Father taught us. Bless mankind with your joy by placing him in the position that he, too, can enjoy life simply by looking at your face. So smile and bring joy back into mankind's heart. Lead him into the Heaven in which you have learned to live on the Earth.

And now, a very simple prayer:

> *"May God bless each man who teaches these words, who listens to them and who tries to fully understand them, for as the Lord walks beside thee each morning of your life, bless Him and thus bring blessings into your life.*   *Amen.*

After listening to you reread these words, we felt in essence that some of the thoughts were perhaps not made as clear as they should be. Mankind does not understand that the Lord has a great love for each man and that He dispenses that love equally. The Father will reward each man in kind if the time is taken to talk with Him in the morning, and if we would take the time to meditate and to listen for the directions and answers He wishes to bring to us. The Lord can and will bless each day for us, which will certainly give life a lot more meaning because it would provide evidence that we are on the pathway we promised originally to follow.

The Lord loves each animal as much as He loves man. He created these animals just as man was created, and those of us who live on the Earth must respect His love for these animals and not--in any manner, shape or form--harm them. We must look at them with love in our hearts as we should look upon man. If man is to survive, he must learn to respect one another; he must learn to love one another. Man has become so selfish that he does not want to share his thoughts. Therein lies the secret of how God's original *Laws* were lost. Mankind was so selfish that they began to substitute other words for the *Original Truths* rather than share them verbatim as they had been taught. As a result, man was educating others so long with the misconceptions that he himself forgot the *Original Laws*.

The Teacher goes on to explain how they have been examining men's minds for centuries and we would like to express this one thought in addition to the lesson: Mankind must come to the conclusion on his own that he cannot live alone. It matters not whether he lives in a hut or a palace, but he must live closely with his fellowman. He can live in a shack. It does not matter to the Father. Mansions are not important. We do not take any of that back with us. We must stop separating ourselves by walls, moats, and any other expressions that distance ourselves from our fellow-man. We must learn to share our emotions and our knowledge. One thing mankind must get straight is that no man can truly live alone without finally finding himself emotionally sick, with a troubled heart and a sad soul because when man was created by God, when He put us down upon the Earth, He said,

> *"If you will live together as I have placed you and care for one another, love one another, and take on the troubles of one another, then truly you shall learn and you shall live the Laws, and you shall return safely back home to Me."*

CLEANLINESS IS NEXT TO GODLINESS
(A Meditation)

On this particular afternoon as I went into my meditation, I found myself sitting by the river bank that I have grown accustomed to visit. Perhaps this is my place of refuge for when I return from meditating there, I always feel composed and at peace with myself and the world.

On this particular afternoon, I saw the vision of huge, rough bark logs floating down the stream and I saw huge boulders obstructing the water from flowing freely, thus inhibiting the logs from going further down the stream. Two thoughts were brought to my mind: I wondered how much energy and light the water would need to overcome the obstacles ahead and beyond. I watched the water wash over the smaller stones and again wondered how hard the water would have to flow to cleanse the minds of man so as to purify them of their negativity, hatred and fear. It was as though the question I heard kept being echoed from river bank to bank: How long would it take a stream of purified water to flow over your minds, to clean them completely of all negativity, all evil, and all hatred?

Then finally came the answer: Hatred flows as easily as the water; so in order to be able to overcome this obstacle—like the huge boulders in the stream—the water must flow even more furiously. To illustrate our thoughts, we wish to add the following: Since our world is filled with both loving and hateful thoughts, we could say hatred can be allowed to flow as easily as the water. However, once man allows hatred to stay in his mind, it becomes hardened like the huge boulders in the stream. Thus in order to wash away hard, stone-like hatred, the stream's flow of loving, positive thoughts would have to intensify greatly. By this realization you can see that man must concentrate even harder to get rid of hatred.

The answer remains with you, my child, and with all of mankind as to how soon man will adjust to feelings of peace and harmony within himself and to extending love to all of mankind.

When my mind felt cleansed of all thoughts, the Master Teacher began telling me that when he first began to understand a little bit about the clutter within man's mind, he immediately instructed them as to how to eliminate hatred and fear from their minds. He taught them that if they loved as fiercely as they hated, there would never be cause for any fear or hatred. He began to show me how hard it was to overcome the burdens men carry today with all of the hatred and fear they have toward one another. He informed me that the one who evolves beyond this state of negative thinking can enlarge the amount of his light by "two-fold." He showed me how to send thoughts of love to all who are ill and to all men that we hated and who hate us in return. He said: *"Send out love to them; do not display any dismay if and when they do not respond in kind. Man's attitude toward man can change if love is directed toward them. Whenever you feel that you dislike someone for something they have done to you or others, try to fill that space in your mind with love."*

The Father allows us to fulfill our destiny each time we live down on the Earth, but the wise man alone seems to care enough, to strive enough, to fulfill his destiny, while the others dawdle about hoping to live again so they can investigate a new life. When man dawdles, the main purpose of being on Earth is forgotten and lost.

During the period of meditation the Master Teachers came back to the topic of ridding ones mind of hatred and negativity over and over. He used every excuse He could find, every illustration He could describe and inserted them into my mind to discourage me from thinking evil or negative thoughts about anyone. If within our minds we feel negativity, we must immediately replace it with thoughts of love and more love.

How many men understand what the word love truly means? These were the questions that I was asked. Do men love themselves? Are they capable then of feeling love for anyone? The Father then continued with the lesson,

> *"Love is a feeling of warmth and exhilaration that you feel totally in every cell of your being—your mind, soul, spirit, heart and in your very being—in every thought that you have. If you can feel My love completely taking over your person, you will then realize that the purpose that man has for coming back to live upon the Earth can be fulfilled."*

After so profound a thought, I thought our conversation was over, but He went on to talk more about the water in the stream. He mentioned that not only was it relaxing to watch the water flow, but that He had made water possible so that mankind could keep themselves clean and replenish the body's needs— *Cleanliness is next to Godliness.* He told me how in the very beginning He had informed us how to keep ourselves clean and that we were to wash ourselves every morning.

He said:

"Watch the birds and catlike animals and see how they preen themselves. So you must do also. You must contain your feces by digging a hole deep, deep into the Earth. In that way you will replenish some of the nutrients which you have used by living off of the Earth. The hole is to be deeply dug away from the water for the rubbish (meaning fecal matters, etc.) was not to enter the water system. Make sure you do not bathe where your drinking water comes from; seek another venue. You must live close to the Earth and learn the lessons that the Earth has to teach you. In so doing, you will be able to overcome every difficulty that keeps you from fulfilling your purpose on Earth.

"Remember, a new life begins every morning. See to it that your body is clean, that your mind is clean also and free from prejudices of any kind, and try to teach and help those who are less fortunate. Remember always to acknowledge that evil can only exist if man allows it to live within himself. So, learn to substitute love for hatred, kindness for meanness, and reach out to all of God's creatures.

Thus ended my meditation and communication with the Master Teacher. I felt reluctant to end it and to arouse myself from this state of pure love.

THOU SHALT LOVE EACH OTHER

As you will recall, it was noted that when the Father took leave of man, He said that man had to love one another with all of his heart and all of his soul, but he did not say we had to like them.[1] The Lord has taught us to love all men, no matter how evil they may appear, no matter if we differ with their judgments. The distinct pleasure of having all men treated equally by each other remains a priority within God's mentality. We must observe and live His *Laws* and treat all men equally since what happens to one man happens likewise to all of mankind.

We must set the example and hope that all men observe and become wiser in their observations.

During each lifetime, many thoughts come back into our minds that remind us of past times. A man very often becomes

---

[1] Love and Like

There is a difference between these words. A mother of an only child came to me for help. She was desperate because of the way her son was living. He had brought shame upon himself and his family. She finally confronted him. "You are my son, and I shall always love you, but I do not like you because of what you represent today. Remember, my Son, there is always a day of reckoning." Her son was visibly shaken. His mother had never criticized him before. Slowly the son did change and became an outstanding citizen.

wiser due to these thoughts. They are recollections of experiences that he has lived through and accomplished. We all have the great desire to want to live on top of the mountain; but if we see the mountain from afar, we may be afraid to climb the mountain. Then we shall never attain the height that we were capable of doing. So it is with life. If we fear every turn and every twist in life, then we cannot attain the wisdom or the height of living and learning. We are opposed to *Truth Everlasting* unless we understand how to use it wisely. As an example: If we fumble the ball--so to speak--do we stoop to pick it up and correct our error or lament the rest of our lives that we let the ball fall? We must turn inward and assume the responsibility of all threats that come into our lives. We then must reclaim that which belongs to us and leave the rest alone.

We each have the ability to sort out fact from fiction and the chaff from the wheat. We also feel rewarded from on high when the Lord blesses us, when we have enough faith to go forward.

We must always look for the signs of upward movement, never downward, because many negative thoughts will be placed into our consciousness as we proceed with our lives and will drag us back to prevent us from reaching our heights. Do not be afraid to live your life; have faith and all will occur in God's time.

PART II

LEARNING HOW TO LIVE ON EARTH

THE LAW OF LOVE

I thought this would be a good time to speak to you about the first *Law* and the greatest *Law*: *The Law of Love*. This is the basic *Law*; from this one first *Law* springs all other *Laws*. The *Law of Love* is vital because it is the basic power of the universe. It is the creative force. If we were to dissect this idea of love, we would discover it is the attraction of one to another. The smallest of molecules is also a part of God. The smallest molecule holds within itself a spark of light, of God's power. God's unsupported wholeness attracts these molecules together and all things are created out of these molecules. We must always comprehend that everything we own in our homes and that we wear are made of basic molecules of various and different vibratory rates. The molecule, although it does not possess a so-called personality nor does it have the ability to discern, still has within it the basic God-power, which is love. So what you might call the holding together of all objects may be described as the attraction through love of one another. Even the smallest things in our universe are held together by this attraction, which is related to and is within the *Law of Love*.

Love is indeed a strange, interesting and fascinating thing and is difficult to define in words or in a scientific manner. It also has an emotional quality within the creatures that has the ability to reason and think. This emotion helps one to be attentive and to be protective of one another. Man considers many animals are not important or intelligent, but these animals--when they sense an enemy approaching--will gather around to protect those who are smaller and more helpless. We are referring to animals like the elk and the reindeer for they will gather in great circles to protect those unable to protect themselves; this is done through the dynamics of love. It is also known that some animals, when they lose their mate, will never mate again or, if they mate once, will never change a mate for another until one or the other is lost because of this law of attraction of love.

Mankind prefers to believe he is so advanced in his training and his thinking. He believes that he and he alone discovered love. That love was indeed for someone of an opposite sex. He feels only man is capable of giving his attention and deep affection for that individual. Sometimes such a union is blessed with children, and so he also extends his love to his family. But you see, man is not as smart as the molecule—for it has no ability to reason. Man does not find himself able to love all of mankind--a law still needed to be learned.

Jesus' Mission on Earth

Remember, my child, Jesus came to Earth primarily for this one mission alone, to teach man the *Law of Love*, and the *Laws of God*. Remember always His words, *"Love ye one another."*

Paul re-emphasized Jesus' words, that Jesus was no different from any other man. Paul told us that we were all part of one another—all members of one big family. There is an instinct that dwells within all of us, a basic desire to love one another, for the God within us--which is *Love*--is yearning to express God's love.

In our vast knowledge and thinking, we have built up the walls that separate black from red, yellow from white, and Jew from Catholic, so we have forgotten what love is all about, and its true meaning.

Paul used another word; he called it "charity." In a way, it is a bit more expressive than the word love, for charity means more than love of one another, but also the giving of one another to another and the sharing of what you have with others. Paul also said that, no matter what might be gained in life, if you had not charity or love, you would have lost everything, including the progression of your soul so what does man profit if he can conquer the whole world but lose his own soul?

The basic *Law of the Universe* is, always has been, and always will be the *Law of Love*.

God is the personification of *Love*!

ALL MEN WERE CREATED AT ONE TIME

The Masters say there really is nothing new in the world, that education is the same in this lifetime as in previous lives. While we, the students, are living on this pathway, thoughts are brought forth today which we believe are original; yet upon further study, we see these thoughtwaves have been with us from the very beginning of time.

We, your Teachers, want to relate this incident of history to you so that you can record it for all mankind to understand.

"All of mankind originated together at the same time. We simultaneously began to live at the exact same time."

You can say, "Why bother to explain the origin of man?" Because man simply does not understand that his true identity, combined with the energy that the Lord left behind for us to use, is the identical energy with which we originated many centuries ago. We want to combine these truthful thoughts, otherwise unknown to mankind, with the missing link of *Truth* sought after by all in the hereafter.

You can see we bring you *Truth* in driblets so that you are able to learn about *Truth Everlasting*. We would like to see men letting the energy flow. They all have ability to hear and to see and feel everything as it was and as it is. For the same energy they originated with, they will return with—hopefully having added more energy by learning and teaching the *Original Truth*.

SEEK YOUR ETERNAL MATE

As I spoke to you the last time and related to you that we were all created at one time, so I wish to continue today.

It all happened at one time; an explosion of thinking occurred within mankind's mind; he found himself surrounded by other men. It was then the Lord spoke out to them and He said, "Within one short moment I shall begin to tell you a story *of Truth Everlasting*. It is the beginning of lessons I will bring on a regular basis."

As we gathered together around His presence, we understood that His light meant for us to gather together in a circle. At first, we sat apart. Then a fire-like object appeared in our midst, and we were directed to sit closer together. This helped to give us an exchange of energy. The soft-spoken voice began to speak:

> *"Remember always to hover close to one another. Clear out your thinking now because I am about to begin lessons that must occupy your minds completely. So sort out any other thoughts you might have. In other words, clear out your minds for My words."*

We waited for Him to begin. All at once, His signaling light danced around in front of us, and we began to feel a bit frightened. Then a hush fell over all of us, and the voice hinted that the fire was raw energy and light, and that we needed to understand light itself. Therefore, we should watch the fire, inhale its fumes, and listen attentively to its thoughts. As He began looking up into the heavens, so did we. Instead of the darkness that had been there before, there suddenly appeared light. Again, a hush fell over us, as we at last understood the greatness of the moment. We sat motionless. Soon He began to speak anew:

"I want you to remember the thoughts of Truth I bring to you continually, on a daily basis. Since you are human, you may forget some of the words, so you must gather and study together. You must repeat the words rigorously so soon you will be anointed with the oils of understanding. If and when you understand these words of Truth which I shall bring to you, you shall have gained the education needed to mount the steps to the Kingdom of Heaven."

The Father fixed His gaze upon us studiously and continued:

"Do not allow your emotions to run wild. Harness your energy and your mind's eye. Curb your thinking of education and allow your minds to freely comprehend My teachings. Say no more mentally to your partner until I have finished. First, gird your loins. You will soon find a mate for yourself. Look around you, search the face and heart of each person until you are endowed with the knowledge of understanding his or her heartaches as much as you do your own. You will then indeed have found the mate you were seeking. You must understand their thinking. Also, look for a mate who understands the evils as well as the good of life and is

willing to share all they know with you."

Then He sent us out to look for that one certain mate. We looked over each other. We disliked some and adored others, and soon the right mate was found. The Lord then told us:

"Say nothing more to your tribesmen until you are sure that this is the mate that you want to live with throughout all eternity. When you have decided together to make a union, greet the Lord and say, 'I do want this mate.' Then go with your mate to the high priest whom I have placed as a member of each tribe. Request of him the solemn oath that you must take, and then announce to all of your tribesmen that this is the mate you have chosen. Then again, you shall greet the Lord, saying, 'Ever will this be my chosen mate, if You so will. For until the end of time, I shall continue to search for my eternal mate and sooner than later he or she may be found again in either the mate I have chosen in this lifetime or the one who awaits me when I step through the door of eternal life.

NOTE: Each person comes to Earth with a mission to fulfill. If one soul mate fulfills his or her mission and the other does not, it does not necessarily mean that these soul mates return together on their next reincarnation. Some may choose to remain on the other side of the veil to better help their mates down on Earth fulfill their mission, hoping those on Earth may eventually reconcile all differences and return safely to fulfill their full and true mission on the other side of the veil.

Each reincarnation does not mean a soul mate returns, but rather other mates are selected to help each other to succeed in fulfilling their original mission. When they return to the other side of the veil, they find their soul mates waiting for them.

The soul mate who chooses not to reincarnate has other steps of higher learning and is striving to grow in higher consciousness and has chosen to be about our Father's business.

Vision

On the evening of December 24, 1995, I had finished editing the chapter titled "Seek Your Eternal Mate." I had the following vision which had puzzled me for several days until that date. During my afternoon meditation, my teacher explained that this had been brought to me so that it could be used as an addendum to the above-mentioned chapter to clarify the subject matter.

In the vision I had dreamt that I was walking on a graveled pathway that was not familiar to me, but I felt comfortable while being there. Suddenly I saw a large white building shaped like a one-story barn or a manufacturing plant. I would later see a large black pipe at least two feet in diameter running from the back to the front of the building about shoulder height. As I approached this building, I saw a tall, handsome blond-haired man standing on the pathway apparently waiting for me to join him. The urge to embrace and kiss him was overwhelming, but somehow I restrained myself thinking, "You are a married woman; how would the onlookers react to this?" Instead of embracing him, I reached out and clasped his hand. No words were spoken, but I could sense his joy at seeing me and he continued to clasp my hand very tenderly as though he didn't want ever to let it go. The feeling I had was that we were lovers and worked together and that he needed my advice or opinion about buying this building.

He motioned to a man who was standing in the doorway of this large white building letting him know that we had arrived and were about to go inside. We walked hand in hand up to the door; it was then that I separated my hand from his. I could feel his disappointment as he looked at me askance wondering or questioning as to why I was not accompanying him into the building. The impression I felt was the building had to do with his ownership of other similar buildings and he was there to negotiate a price for this one. It would then allow him to own all of this type building which created some type of energy that was useful to mankind. Since not one word was spoken, the impressions were all done mentally. I suddenly awakened-- never seeing this loved one again.

Meditation

My Teacher explained that the young man whom I had so wanted to embrace and kiss when I first saw him had been my husband when we had lived on the other side of the veil before I came back to live on the Earth again. They continued to explain that someday when I had finished all of my mission on Earth, I would be allowed to return to my life on the other side of the veil.

> *"You see my child, this episode proves there is continued life after one passes through the veil, that unless all of your missions are completed, we must reincarnate again to finish the parts left undone. It also reiterates and confirms my Teacher's lessons about both of the soul mates not necessarily reincarnating at the same time.*

THE TRUTH

Once upon a time, there was a man who set sail to see the Father. He sought out the Father and said, "Extol me, O Lord God, Father of the Universe, for am I not a Lord?" But the Father responded:

> *"No. I am the King over the beasts, the animals, mankind and Truth. If I allow myself to extol a Lord, then the King would be remiss, for I am the sole survivor of the knowledge of Truth."*

Mankind refuses to understand that the dogma that is being taught today is considered by the Father--as well as our Masters, Teachers and Guides--as being less than truthful. In the beginning of time before God set us free on the Earth, He would instruct us with Lessons of *Truth* that would make our lives easier, simpler, more complete and, in the end, would safely guide us back to Him. Mankind refused to understand the importance of these lessons and, no matter how many times they were repeated to him, man often would argue and question the Father as to the significance of the lesson. When the Father explained patiently to them that it was necessary for them to listen intently and be able to recall each word exactly as He had taught them, they still stubbornly refused to listen attentively.

Since men expected the *Laws* to be something very difficult to learn and understand, the simplicity of the *Truths* that the Father was teaching them, therefore, could not be important in their minds. So they would take His words and repeat them in their own fashion, adding to them, deleting from them and at one time one of the men said, "Let us divide this lesson into four parts. You learn one part; another the second part, and so on." But little did they know that one man would depart from the immediate vicinity before the other three, and so one of the parts would also be missing from the complete lesson.

The Lord spoke out to them so many times that He finally became so offended by their indifference that He no longer met with them. Instead, He sent to them a messenger who tried to reiterate the lessons of *Truth* the Father had tried to inculcate into their minds. But they argued and resented the messenger, saying, "We refuse to accept any lessons of any so-called *Truth* from anyone except the Father." And so the messenger returned to the Father, feeling he had failed in his mission.

When he reported to the Father what had happened and that he had been rebuffed by the men, the Father praised him for his efforts, but within Himself He thought, *"Perhaps I should send another messenger; perhaps he will be more capable of teaching them in a different manner."* He called unto Himself one of His most learned Teachers and requested that he go to meet with the men to see if he could teach them. That wise Teacher went forward and was likewise rebuffed and ridiculed in the same manner as the first Teacher. The men refused to accept any of his teachings, saying again, "Unless the Father presents Himself to us and teaches us, we refuse to listen to your lessons."

The Father then presented Himself before the men for the last time before they were set free upon the Earth, and He informed them that they were to be set free upon the Earth with their own free will. He directed:

"You shall remain alive upon the Earth and roam the face of the Earth until you have mastered every word of My original Teachings. I have sent you two of My most learned Masters and you have refused to listen to them. I have repeated My Laws to you over and over again, but you persist in interpreting them in your own manner and

you have refused to accept the significance of their meaning. So now you shall not again see My face until you have finished your quest of living on the Earth and you have learned My Laws.

"In My parting words I say to you again: You are to live together; you are to be responsible one for the other; you are to treat each other as you would have yourself treated; and you shall love your fellowman with all your heart and with all your soul. And this I say unto thee: you shall remain alive on the Earth until you have learned and lived My Laws."

A PRAYER TO GOD

"Almighty God, blessed Master over all of us, educate us further into the Universal Laws that You deem necessary for us to learn before returning home. Almighty Father, please educate us more pertinently so we might understand how to live our present day-to-day life. We deem it a necessity as well as a privilege to learn the steps necessary to enable us to understand the Laws and Life Everlasting. We deem it a privilege and pleasure to state unequivocally that we know that You do not condone the so-called Truths we are being taught today on the Earth. We plead with You to further educate us along Your line of thinking to be able to know Thy pathway, so we may understand how to elevate our consciousness. Please educate us in such a fashion, Almighty Father, that we might be able to live nearer to Thee. Amen"

We, your Teachers, answer your plea and prayer.

The answer is a simple one: Learn to alter your consciousness more and more through meditation and prayer. All will be made known to you at the proper time and in the proper sequence.

You have, been taught, *"Thou shalt not hate thy fellowman and Thou shalt not kill thy fellowman."* Many men seem to find it difficult at times to remember and to live by these thoughts today. We, your Teachers, beseech you to align your mind with God's *Laws* and use your abstruse or deeper sense of thinking. That is the part of the mind that man uses little.

It is when you use your abstruse sense that the Lord God Almighty can set into motion thoughts of *Truth* worth learning. When you do touch upon the *Universal Laws*, that are so deeply rooted in your higher mind and so little used today, you have the ability to at that moment in time to recall the laws that you have learned through many past lifetimes.

What do we mean by that? Well, occasionally we set thoughts into motion, thoughts found within the memory bank; we set them free in order to advance farther into the *Universal Laws* bank so to speak. Lest we confuse you further, we wish to tell you there are many memory banks in man's mind. The

Universal Law memory bank is one, and it is the most neglected by men who now live on mother Earth. It seems man has lost the ability and knowledge of how to enter that bank and use its knowledge. It is like being able to withdraw monies that you have deposited into a saving account. Man certainly does not forget about that commercial bank on Earth! It seems, my child, that man uses his knowledge so lightly that he never seems to try to think deeply about any subject. If we indulge him with a new thought or *Law*, it seems to interfere with his private life and thinking. Man does not want to think about the price he might have to pay for his excesses in life. "I'll just enjoy life today; maybe I will think about the moral and ethical *Laws* tomorrow." Man seldom thinks about *Truth Everlasting*; seldom does He think of living any other place than on the Earth. Again he will not allow himself to think that life can end and that he will go back owing. Thus, he never pressures his mind to recall anything stored in his memory bank. Because of this, man loses or occludes from his mind that actuality of remembering thoughts from the near past. He likewise fails to consider the future tense. Man has memory loss.

Use Your Mental Processes

How do we advance this theory or idea—that man has a right to jolt his memory bank into action or to assert his will upon different memory banks? You ask, "How do we assert our will upon the mental processes?"

A good start would be to study the cause and effect of our efforts in this lifetime. Do we ever do that? Seldom do we question our minds by asking how we are doing, or what is meant for us to be accomplishing during this lifetime. If we do not use access to our mindset, it simply means that we limit our knowledge both here and in our next experience. If we occasionally think a thought about our purpose on Earth and how we are progressing, it should result in jolting our mind setting into motion our ability to remember our true state of being. Assessing the knowledge of why we are here on Earth at this time, what mission have we chosen, are we succeeding in our mission or are we totally off the pathway. We could and should learn how to use the 'cause and effect' ideas and attitudes to strengthen those memory banks and help us evaluate the answers to the above questions.

The prayers asking God to help solve every little problem that presents itself was not meant to be used every day. It is only meant to relieve troubles and problems after searching deeply for answers within our own minds. If we cannot come up with an answer, then we should seek the Lord's ideas as to how He would suggest we handle a certain problem, trial, or tribulation. Access to the Father is meant for a purpose, not relegated only to having an exchange of thoughts. The Father encourages us only to seek Him out when we are in dire need. Otherwise, He feels we are capable of jolting our memory banks and seeking the answers to personal trials and tribulations.

In other words, my child, seek answers to your troubles by being dependent upon your memory bank. Do not call upon the Father for every solution that you need on a daily basis. Learn to use your memory bank often, and use it wisely and well.

Access yourself often by asking, "How am I doing?" "Where am I going?" "Am I fulfilling my goals?" "Am I growing in consciousness?" If you are truthful to yourself in your evaluations, you are then assessing your failures, your faults, and your successes. Therefore, you are not seeking a scapegoat to handle the necessary errors that you make down on Earth. You are taking personal responsibility for your acts. The Lord does not sit in judgment every moment. He assesses us only when we safely return home to Him. He does not keep a daily worksheet on our errors. He is a loving Father, and He gives us a chance time and time again to change our form of living and thinking. In His assessment of our abilities to handle our daily trials and tribulations, He asks that we do our very best, jogging our memory banks for knowledge. He does not say that we cannot use our higher consciousness to contact Him. He wishes for us to depend upon our consciousness to enlarge it so in that way we become able to alleviate many of our daily problems.

Another way to assess your growing consciousness is to ask yourself this question: Do you defer to yourself when you are in trouble, or do you run to God right away with your laments and heartaches and accuse him of ruining your life here on Earth? Do you access yourself and the situation first before contacting Him, or do you bless yourself enough that He does not have to bless you? You see, my child, it is a simple process to appraise oneself and accept the blame for all the wrong things, accepting the responsibility of everything upon our own shoulders. "Lay it on me Father, I deserve more than the trials and tribulations that have been given me. They have not been harsh enough. I deserve more punishment than you have given me at the present time."

Do you access yourself prudently, or do you feel knowledgeable enough to say to the Father, "I have sinned, but I am trying awfully hard to change and to atone for my sins alone. I do not blame You or any man for what has happened to me."

Acknowledge your faults, yes, but do not bind yourself within them. Acknowledge your positive traits also to stimulate your progress. Remember that this is the way of His *Laws* and His love.

HARVESTING

Harvesting the Father's Lessons

We recall when the Lord, blessed be His name, came to us to inform us that we must learn when to harvest the wheat:

"You must harvest the wheat when the weather permits, given that rain shall occasionally fall during your lifetime, but learn to salute Me each morning and follow

My instructions exactly as I advise. You will know when to harvest the wheat."

At that time, He had informed us that He would not teach us the *Laws* in any certain order, or whether they related to one another really did not matter. What was more important was that we were to follow the *Laws* to the nth degree. He gave them to us so that our lives would be made more simple. He advised us that if we followed His admonitions, our lives would not be fraught with pain and anger and that we should always be able to let go of grudges rather than to hold on to them. He advised us to bless each person no matter how deep the hurt, bless them with happiness and joy. He again advised us to put aside all negative thoughts and not allow them to linger in our minds to grow roots, so to speak; that if we did, we would bring pain into our own lives. In this fashion, He had advised us to execute, extricate and be rid of each and every thought of fear, hurt and negativity. No one can help us with this duty; we must do it alone.

We must understand that with all of the neglect of the Lord by man He has controlled His planning without heaping vengeance upon all of us during all of these centuries. Why can we not see that we should follow in His mold? Why do we constantly carry hatred and deter ourselves from perfection while all we have to do is follow His pattern of *Truth Everlasting?*

THE FIRST MAN RETURNED

(A Parable)

"Help us, O Heavenly Father, help us understand Your lessons. Help us to understand the depth of Your thinking from the very beginning of time until the very end. Help us, O Father; have mercy in Your heart and help us find our way back to Thee. Amen"

The first man was sent out with directions as to how to find his way back home. The second man was given the same directions as the first, but there was no way to foresee nor account for what would happen.

During the night while the second man slept, a mudslide occurred which prevented him from using the directions. He became hopelessly lost. He tried all different directions, only to proclaim he was just plain lost. He kept wandering aimlessly; he hoped against hope that the first man would send help for him when he had not returned on schedule. After awhile, a third man was sent out with the original directions which had been the *Original Truths* and had been given to the first man as well as the second. The third man also became hopelessly lost because of the mudslide, but he did meet the second man. Though they tried many different ways, they decided that there was no way they would ever find their way back home.

The first man was then sent out again. He appeared before the two lost men with what appeared as new directions, but actually they were the original ones that had been given to them. He then realized that the second and third men had become lost because they had not properly interpreted the directions on the same level as the first man. You see, the first man had used his imagination and ingenuity on a higher level; thus, he was able to find his way back easily. He had been sent forth as the fourth man and he had helped to find the two lost men. He continued to talk with them; he continued to show them how to elevate their consciousness and thus explore different avenues by reading between the lines not merely to understand what was on the lines. He continued to teach them to observe other constructive thoughts until finally they understood how to find their way back.

This information that they learned was not ever told by them to any man who was to follow in their footsteps or follow their pattern of living. The men continued to salute the Lord each morning, but they never again alluded to His helping them. Though they greeted Him each morning in prayer, they soon forgot how to thank Him for His help. It was their arrogance that did not allow them to admit even to themselves that it was not a sin to get lost on life's pathway, but a sin if they did not try to learn why they were lost, and so they continued to refuse to accept the positive directions offered to them by the Father. They could easily have informed other men who went forth that they did not have to hide their heads in shame and fear even though they might get lost on the Earth. That even if they did get lost, it did not have to be forever—that if man tried hard to find his direction, the Father would eventually help him find his way back home. This is the positive direction which man should take with the Father's guidance, and it could be easily done if man would only listen carefully to the directions which the Father brings to him each morning. Thus the opposite occurred--and because of their arrogance and false pride, they lived negative lives.

Until this very day, there are those who continue to teach man about hell and damnation, charging them to find the Father alone and saying there is no help for them on the Earth unless they do exactly as the false ministers direct. So, now you realize how distortions started with man.

GOD IS WITHIN US

The Father is like the tree in a forest. The Father stands close by saying to us:

"Look straight ahead, My children; see the trees ahead in the forest. Look at a particular tree. Observe it well for it is like Me. Once you learn to greet Me and gather My love and energy around you, so you will be able to see Me in all of mankind, just as you see the similarities in the trees of the forest. If you look ahead, you will always be able to see Me protecting all of mankind from evil. The reason that I have the mist facade around Me is to protect Myself from evil as well."

This is one of those lessons on *Truth Everlasting* that emphasizes teaching man to continue to look for and to live close to the Father and each other. We must teach each man to say to himself: *"My Father, watch over me until the end of time so that at that time I shall be close to Your divine face. Amen.*

Let us continue what we started this morning and know that He is within us.

Our thoughts are His thoughts. He reveals the mysteries of the universe to us.

Men should learn to adore the Lord and accept Him as though He were beside them. Accept Him. Learn the meaning of those words and let Him in. Let Him know that you want His presence about you and within you by accepting His *Truths*. You must learn to defer to Him by admitting to yourself that His will is more important than your own. So, when your mind is free, say these words to Him:

"Almighty Father, Blessed Angel of Truth, include me in Your daily thoughts. Excuse me; forgive me if I do not praise you enough. I stare off into space not knowing the Truth that You are there also. I speculate upon the mysteries of the universe; yet, I do not have to speculate because You relate them and explain all of the so-called mysteries to me. Why then do I not relate these things-- these mysteries--of Your thinking? Should I not recognize Your thoughts as equal unto mine? Should I not understand that my thoughts are indeed Your thoughts from the very beginning? Amen"*

We hope that you will allow us to experiment a little bit with your thinking this morning. We want you to visualize the Lord God Almighty, who is the Father over all of us, standing nearby. Each man should visualize the Lord as he imagines Him to be. In His presence we are not cowed. We are elated because the showering of His attention upon us proves to us how much He loves us and cares about our being here on the Earth. In accordance with this thinking, we educate our minds to live humbly on this pathway called a lifetime. We listen each morning to what our inner voice tells us of His guidance and direction. We know in advance how to apply our minds to triumph over a travail that we might have to face. We entrust our lives into His hands. We, as humans, have visions of evil and negativity around us, but He does not allow anything untoward to occur to us. His vigilance is ever present. He always lives with mercy in His heart. After a while He raises the ante, so to speak. He asks us to refrain from living in a pattern that would lead us down the road to destruction. He asks only that we resume the position of trust in which we had been placed in the beginning of time. It enables us to succeed in the now. The trust and faith which we have in Him allows us to occasionally call upon Him for help, but we should always first try to work things out alone before calling for His help. We can do this by using our altered state of mind--meditation. It helps us to succeed in learning the answers. If we rely on the Father constantly, it could cause Him loss of energy. We must remember that, as any good parent who wants to lighten his child's load at any cost, we can too often use His light which He so willingly offers. We, too, must have mercy upon Him and His beloved Angels by allowing them to know that we can help ourselves, that we have grown in stature, and that we can live alone for short periods of time. It also helps the Angels to regroup and regenerate as we do when we meditate, rest or sleep.

We humans use too much energy analyzing and re-analyzing things we cannot change. Let it be! Tomorrow is another day! So man made a mistake. We must not hang him out to dry because of it. We must allow our minds to forgive and forget and start the new day right. By saying nothing to the person who erred, you are allowing him to remove his shirt of sackcloth. Incriminating each person for each error uses up much of our own energy. Then it allows your load to become too heavy to carry, and illness is the result. So tell them to stop rehashing and rehashing things they cannot change. Instead, ask for God's help and His blessings.

LAWS

Good morning. We have gathered here today to try to explain certain parts of the *Laws* that are not being adhered to in our present-day society. Each person should be allowed equal time to express themselves. A teacher should not have special or favorite students. We as Teachers often disagree among ourselves and we appreciate the time given us to explain our points of view. We have always tried to identify and express justice for all, but we lament the fact that not one of us seems to possess the ability to assess justice correctly. What one of us might feel conclusively within ourselves as being a form of justice, there can be ten different reasons why our conclusions are inconclusive.

Do you understand that we strive to educate and thus to help man understand the troubles that each endures? We must all try to have compassion for every man, no matter his origins, his creed or his color. Do we not all have troubles? History teaches us that human troubles and ills have been present throughout all eternity. Some of us seem to be able to express ourselves a bit more articulately than others and justice is then meted out in our favor; but that is not the Father's *law of equality and justice* for each man.

We must inculcate into our mind one of the *Laws* and that is: *do <u>not</u> allow <u>evil</u> or <u>negativity</u> to be part of our lives.* If you will observe man today, you will note that he is beset by troubles and negativity. It is as though he has never heard of this *Law*. We are dwelling upon this subject because we would like the man who tries to live in the light to teach these *Truths* to one another in the way plain folks educate each other down on the farms. For example, in the country they try to help one another learn how to live and prosper along side of each other without jealousy or resentment of one another. They understand they must all pull together to survive. They educate each other when to gather in the harvest, when to plant the seeds; and that if they do not harvest in time the crops could be ruined by rain or sudden freeze. Realizing they cannot control weather problems, they have learned to live with the laws of nature. Thus, they have a private pact that is unspoken but understood among themselves. They realize how they must live and work together for their common survival. Who among them would be foolish enough to think they could survive alone? No one. Education is like a harvest of foodstuffs: if you do not learn how to use your mind adequately, there never will be a time for harvest. Thus, we say to you: study the *Universal Laws* and propositions that we are allowed to bring to you these days. Study all the principle ideas that are sent forth amid us so that we might survive together.

First, we must observe the law of living together, understanding one another's needs and reaching out to help the one in need. Needless to say, there are differences among us from birth time on, but who of us can stand alone at birth? Do we not have to learn to crawl about in this lifetime before we can stand on our own two feet? Do we not relinquish control over our bodies to those who care for us when we are first born? It is too bad that as we mature, we imagine or fear that we are completely forsaking control over our independence when we first rely upon someone else to help us. Yet that type of thinking about helping one another has kept us living successfully together, helping us to truly understand the original *Universal Laws* and why we must sincerely care for one another.

What kind of Teachers and Guides would we be if we only ascertained those future events that were about to happen that would adversely affect you? Pretty negative don't you think? Doesn't it make sense to also warn you to help you survive? Would it mean that you had forsaken control over your independence? Would you prefer to rely on your own intellect without a warning signal or to be able to survive and fulfill that which you came to do? So it is, my child, when we agree to disagree over certain thoughts; it is to provide you with both sides of the story so that your mind can reach its own decision.

Would that we could impress upon each man's mind that we allocate much time for him to listen to us in order to gain knowledge, wisdom and guidance. Would that they understand how to extend themselves further in their meditation so that they could travel deeper into that part of the mind that is not being used. Every morning upon first arising, if they would allow us just a few moments, we could insert much energy and knowledge into their minds that would assist them during their daytime activities. Though we are not allowed to live man's life, we strive to help man make his life more complete and less complicated so that he might fulfill his mission on Earth.

LEARN FROM THE SEAMAN
(A Parable)

Once upon a time, there was a chance meeting between a merchant seaman and a master seaman. They had served together at one time on one of their voyages. The seaman spoke thusly: "Once I met you upon the high seas when you were the master skipper and I but a plain seaman. It did not matter to you that I was a plain seaman for you thought us all wise men. You knew and understood that we were capable and desirous of helping you find your way back home."

The master skipper greeted the seaman cordially and acknowledged their previous meeting. He asked, "Has your new skipper helped you or allowed you to help him find the way home?"

"No," the seaman replied, "the master of this ship relies on no one. He sent us forth to learn the ways of the sea. He wanted us to know how vast the ocean was and how deep. It seemed unending to all of us. Only at that time when he foresaw turmoil approaching on the sea did he allow the commissioned officers to take charge of our destinies. We found it revolting for we seamen alone knew all the avenues of retreat in case of a stormy sea, but the newly commissioned officers relied only upon their book learning to find the right direction. You see, they had never experienced a storm at sea so instead of running straight into the eye of the storm, they put us about. In putting us about, they overturned the ship and so many able men were lost."

The lesson we must learn from this story is that not all masters of our ships can appreciate our true value. Indeed they could have learned much from the simple seaman, but instead their arrogance lost many lives.

So it is now throughout the world that many of the people know more than the leaders, but their knowledge is never asked for and never ever used.

TRUTH AND IMMORTALITY BELONG TO US

This morning we greet you with a great deal of love. So, let us be about our Father's work.

It is important when we speak of *Truth* that we can understand what is meant by the word "*Truth*." Can man see *Truth*? Can mankind hold a *Truth* in his hands, so to speak? Should he be able to teach *Truth* diligently to his family as well as to all of mankind? What is Truth? Who will listen? A direct result of this type of thinking leads us to realize that we have to search internally within the crevices of our minds and hopefully come to some of the understandings that the prophets taught us centuries ago.

Let us commence with an original *Truth* and investigate it thoroughly. Commence with the thought of "equality." We have always been taught that all men were created equal. For example, there are single men and married men: Single men need to know how married men live. They must know the pluses and minuses because the married man and the single man do not lead equal lives. Since they are created equal, does it not seem to beckon to them to emulate their father and their fathers before them?

Since equality extends into the regions of each man's mind, (let us equate the meaning of "*Truth*" the same way), if man can manifest his own equality through his mind, should he not be able to maintain his own well being as well? They say that there exists a compromise within mankind's own mind. If he prays and blesses the Lord each morning, if he wishes to be aided each day of his life, he can find his own solutions and solve his own problems during this lifetime. If he defers his own opinions, listens to others and hesitates to explain or totally understand his own opinions, he is refusing to think deeply enough to get his own answers thereby allowing interference by others to totally disrupt his life. His salvation, then, would be to enumerate to others only the thoughts of *Truth* that have been active in his mind--even though he does not understand them completely himself. When man relinquishes control of his mind to others it becomes an obstacle. Each man must seriously ponder this because by relinquishing control of his mind, man aborts his true mission on Earth. Does not environment count?

When the Father instills thoughts into man's mind, does He instill the simple thoughts of basic living that man once understood completely? Does man hamper his own life by avoiding the basic concepts of living together? He understood this completely at one time. If man absolves his own mind of negativity, fear and envy, he can manifest his own *Truth* that comes forth from within. Otherwise, he will linger on in this confused state of mind for centuries.

If man relies completely upon himself without consulting with his higher self and the Father, he observes only the Earthly truth that he believes to be truth--which is not necessarily the real *Truth*. That is not exactly what we set out to do. In the beginning of time, we lent our light to mankind to help him seek deeper meaning in this lifetime. We taught him to salute the Lord each morning and to accept the advice that was given as was needed by him to bring out the best of each day during his entire life. It seems reasonable to us, but if man thinks that he maintains control over his own life and no longer needs to seek the Father's advice or guidance, then we (his Teachers and guides) have not impressed him correctly nor succeeded in using our light correctly. We have failed to teach him the importance of remaining connected to the Father's Light and Love--he must then return to live again on Earth.

Now, to continue along these lines on the subject of Truth and Immortality, the title was brought to us during the usual amount of meditative thinking by the Father's apostles. Yes, He continues to have apostles as He did when He lived among mankind. At that time we used His advice easily and completely each morning without question. He advised each man not only to salute Him but to salute himself as well as all men. *"For do I not abide within you?"* He would tell men to salute themselves, *"Say God of my fathers, educate me each day as to how to sustain my life during this lifetime, teach me to be able to face what lies ahead of me."*

Many men face many holocausts due to their own faults. They cease to listen for the Father's advice about living close to Him. *"Allow Me to live within your minds,"* He advised. *"If you allow Me to live within your mind, I can only advise you how to live your daily life."* It matters not what has happened in one's present or past lifetimes. Only today counts.

So let us begin anew each morning, for it is truly a new beginning. Salute the Lord and say:

> *"I will listen more carefully to that which You advise me to do, and I shall continue to love You with all my heart throughout all eternity."*

THE ANCIENT TEACHINGS ARE WITHIN US

As we have told you many times, within each man's mind there still remains all of the ancient teachings which the Father originally deposited into our minds. He had hoped we would be able to recall all of these lessons and, therefore, have the knowledge and ability to place ourselves on top of the mountain close to Him. Few men, however, fully understood the meaning of His teachings. What He gave us was meant for us to remember on high and in the depths of our being and thinking. He said that He had intended to use our minds in the way fishermen use nets to hold onto the fish and for us to hold onto His thoughts.

He told us that if we would remember these lessons, it would lift us out of our own doldrums and would help us to elucidate new ideas into our minds. We sat and waited for thoughts to come into our minds, but He reminded us that it was not that simple; we were obliged to play a part in this drama. We, in turn, had to teach every man that we met down on Earth. If we encumbered ourselves only in doing that, we would be able to remain alive to finish our mission. We also had to use His light and His lessons correctly. Little did we know at the time that *Truth Everlasting* would escape our minds after a very short period of time once He had placed us on the Earth.

We had hoped He could renew this information constantly by educating us as we moved along our pathway, but He was true to His word. He did not return to us. He did send Teachers of *Truth* and messengers to help us remember His teachings.

There were eleven laws He had taught us, and He emphasized that we were to use them to help other men. He wanted us to also teach these laws diligently unto our children. He insisted that we have mercy upon all of mankind. He also advised us to use these laws to alleviate mankind's suffering, and He has proven to us that when we reach out to help others He indeed relieves our suffering in return. We felt He would do so forever, but when He transplanted us to the Earth, we felt separated from Him and because of our human frailties we began to question His *Laws* and *Truths*. Problems began almost immediately for many of the tribes began to settle elsewhere; they did not remain together as He had taught us to do. We remembered only the simple phrases, but not all of the *Laws* since we had become scattered about. We lost touch with one another; and until this present date and time, we still have not communicated with all of the men who started living on the Earth at one time. We still have to learn the original *Truths*; we have to remain alive forever on the Earth through reincarnation until we fully recall and relearn the wisdom of the ages that He taught us long ago. As we mentioned before, the evidence of these ancient teachings of *Truth* remains alive within mankind today.

THE ORIGINAL LAWS

The Teachers cannot understand why mankind will not allow himself to be exceptional. Yet they do know that exceptional people are often ridiculed by the masses on Earth.

But if you allow this element to interfere in your life, you are accepting their problems, their negativity. You must not allow a few men to drive you away from mankind. In other words, you are not allowed to live alone within yourself. You must always seek to live within the parameters of the Golden Rule, that is, the *Laws* that the Father taught each and every one of us.

We are going to begin to teach you these *Laws* a few at a time, and we would like to see you explain them to those who claim they want to live in the light.

A. **THE FIRST LAW** is that we have to live close to one another without reservation, having no negative thoughts about any man. You see, my child, there were no evil men in the beginning. The evil thoughts man has learned came from those who felt that they understood God's Laws better. Their mistaken interpretations led to the downfall of many men. Men listened to these so-called authorities instead of their own instincts that had been given to them by the Father. Remember, we cannot always see the good that is within man, but there is indeed a good streak in each of us; many times we cannot see or understand this good, but we must remember and always make allowances for each man. Remember: God is within.

B.   **THE SECOND LAW** is that each man is responsible for dispensing all of his learning and the sharing of his lessons, as has been taught him by the Father. In turn, the recipient must show that he loves all men just as the Father does not differentiate one man from another. Therefore, each man is responsible for sharing with those who understand and live in the light. This law is extolled in *"Love ye one another."*

C.   **THE THIRD LAW** that we are going to give you today is to illustrate how hard it is for mankind to live alone. If we see someone helpless or in need, we must pray for him in such a manner as to imagine him standing on top of the mountain close to the Lord. In this type of prayer we are sending him healing and love; and at the same time, we are explaining our art of healing to the helpless ones. He will be made happy by imagining himself standing close to the Lord. What we are trying to say to you is that, no matter how badly you may feel or how little you may have, you must share with those who are less fortunate or more helpless than yourself.

LIVE IN HONOR NOT SHAME

As we greet you this morning my child, we are happy to see that you feel light of heart for the first time this week.

Men have adored the Lord God Almighty from the beginning of time immemorial. We understood that He had vanished from our sight in order to teach us about *Truth Everlasting*. In the very beginning He lived among us. We could see His light and features plainly. He directed our every move, action and thought. We depended upon Him for everything. Each of us is to learn in his own way and at his own rate of thinking. It was not meant as a punishment--His leaving us. It was meant rather as an edict to learn *Truth*, the *Almighty Truth*, and to learn how to reason on our own.

Happiness and joy comes only to those who seek after them. If we understand the Father's *Laws* and *Truths*, then joy and happiness are simple to embrace. The Father always uses our light wisely, and in doing so He helps us by demonstrating those *Truths* which we were taught. In our reaching out and helping our fellowman, the Father decides which of His *Truths* are most appropriate for the present moment or task at hand. Many men are not quite ready for certain *Truths*, and the Father is the best to judge at which time these *Truths* should be taught. Man must dedicate this lifetime to educating all human beings. That is the major part of every man's mission. It matters not who they are, where they were reared, not their color nor creed. God says, *"It matters not the man's color, creed or nationality. There is time and space for all."* If man is willing to learn, we are obligated to teach and to reach out and help. This is due all mankind because no man needs to feel or believe that he is inferior to another. We also want to reiterate at this time that no man needs to be in need of food or clothing while the rest of the world lives in luxury. The Father knows that man does not help enough, that man becomes too complacent in thinking only of his personal needs, forgetting about the less fortunate of his fellowman. Man forgets also to teach and offer his knowledge once he becomes successful. Man should start classes in his own group of less fortunates with the title of......................"The Steps I Took to Find Happiness and Joy." We should try to teach each man to endow himself with God's light and banish fear and negativity from his sight and thinking. We feel it is necessary to clarify this a bit more. We are recognizing that unless help is meted out correctly to the recipient so that he recognizes and wants to learn to help himself, our help will not benefit him. He needs to rise above his present state of thinking, education and living and become aware that he cannot become dependent on this help. Help is only to be offered for an interim period of time, only long enough to help man lift himself up.

Children, we want you to remember the purpose of this message and dissertation: It was meant for you to recognize the fact that the Lord dwells within each man on a daily basis. Thus, the object of this lesson on *Truth Everlasting* is to cause man to understand that no one can deny the fact that he owes the Lord more today than yesterday, and that we all owe Him a similar amount of respect and love each moment that He allows us to live upon the Earth.

What does the Lord ask of us? He commands us to bless Him, to shout from the rooftops, "The Lord loves me!" He exults in every life and He wants all men to understand His *Laws* and *Truths*. "He wants us to have mercy in our hearts, love justice and walk humbly in His light."

In accordance to our teachings, the Master or Teacher who receives the most light is the Master or Teacher allowed to educate mankind in *Truth Everlasting*. There is no Master or Teacher whom the Father does not love, but the excess of His light goes to those who seek to help men lift up their heads from shame to honor. The Lord thus saith, *"The lonely man who tries to live within himself deserves as much attention as those who flock around Me and know Me on a daily basis."*

The Father is determined to find and help those men in need of happiness and *Truth*. A long time ago, He stood before us and pledged a sort of allegiance to us, saying, *"I shall always follow your progress if you will simply abide by My Laws and rule with an iron fist when it comes to determining right from wrong."*

Today living down on Earth, you will find men who are in need and who live with shame as well as men who are prosperous and living with honor. You are responsible in seeking out both the men with honor as well as the disreputable ones and teach them equally. Many who live in honor need as much advice as those living with shame. Offer your advice freely to those in need as well as those who live with honor. Say to him who is in need, "Lift up your head to the Lord and proclaim Him your Master Teacher this day. Accelerate your thinking about changing your life." Bless the Lord, saying "Oh Father, I am so in need of Your blessings. I am desperate about my life and want to change it. Will You please help me?" You then shall see His precious light shining down into your mind, and your head shall brim and burn with new ideas--helping to teach you how to lift your head and relearn the *Truths*. Thus, when you live His *Truths*, you live in splendor and honor. In the same manner, all of mankind who live with love of the Lord in their hearts enjoy life forever.

The one lesson we earnestly wish you would learn from this particular teaching is that mankind should always love and believe in the Lord. In so doing, it helps you establish the precedent of loving your fellowman. You cannot truly believe and have faith in the Lord without having that precious love building in your hearts.

PRESENT-DAY MEN

How wonderful to awaken to such a beautiful day! Man needs to bless the Lord for all the beauty He provides. Now, let us get busy.

Present-day men continue to try to destroy themselves. They want to follow the destructive pattern of past generations by generating that same type of energy. Future generations will abhor the men who live today. They will stand in total disbelief that past generations destroyed themselves by not following the teachings of the Lord.

Present-day men do not understand that the *Divine Way* is the only way to save themselves. Erstwhile would they have continued to live like this if they had understood God's teachings? Man understands nothing about *Truth* today. He extols garbage—his material worth! That which man considers important, such as his material assets, will certainly have no value when he returns back *Home*. The trappings so proudly worn today mean nothing on the exchange level of evil for good.

It seems to us that absolutely nothing has much meaning to

man today but his materialistic thoughts. By constantly having his mind absorbed with these materialistic thoughts, man has destroyed his own imagination and original thinking process. He keeps his mind so cluttered with his trappings that he has forgotten that nothing is worth much in material value unless it has exchange qualities.

Who living on the Earth today has the ability to stand close to the Lord and in all truthfulness and honesty extol his own virtues. Obviously, today man's idea of what he values most has less value than anyone thought.

BE HUMBLE—ASK GOD FOR HELP
(A Parable)

Today we have decided to take the time to express ourselves more about *Truth Everlasting*.

The trouble begins with mankind when he tends to obliterate *Truth* from his memory, hoping to slant the *Truth* to mean something else. You see my child, if he can forget *Truth*, he does not have to live in a *Truthful* manner. However, this exposes his backside to trouble also. Fortunately, he has a constitution that allows negativity to regurgitate itself over and over until the dismal smell of *Truth* becomes ambrosia to him. Thus you see, we describe the way man's negative side of himself shows itself until finally accessibility to his kind and noble side rises to the forefront, guiding him to behave appropriately in accordance with *Truth Everlasting*.

In the beginning of this lesson, we promised to relate a story to you about *Truth Everlasting*. Once there was a man who lived on the Earth. He wanted above all else to amass a fortune of *Truths*. We were not allowed to teach him one *Truthful* thought. So all that he amassed he gathered through his own mind and from fellow travelers whom he met on this journey through this life. Occasionally, when he would find one thread of *Truth,* he would elucidate that thread until he manufactured a whole concoction equal to a lesson of *Truth* as the Lord had once taught us. Then one day he looked behind himself, and there stood the August Figure of the Lord. He hailed the Lord with this quote: "Oh Father, have mercy upon my kind and benevolent soul, for surely You can see I have threads of *Truth* which I have been preoccupied with since the day I returned to the Earth."

The Lord looked upon him in a benevolent countenance and as He stood before the man He answered:

"You have cursed yourself doubly for asking Me to salute you. My fellowman, have you not learned the Truth that the Almighty Father, The Benevolent One, stands before you only once during this lifetime? Why have you not asked Him for a lesson of Truth instead of trying to present Him this Truth which you alone have concocted from threads? Do you not realize that you could have had One Real, Whole Truth?"

The August Figure of the Lord disappeared and the man stood there alone, without hope in his heart. He had learned his lesson too late, as most men living on the Earth learn their lessons--too late.

Man Faces Temptations on the Earth

You see, temptations come forth and send man into a tailspin. They observe little of the Lord's *Laws;* they seek instead only self-gratification. Selfishly, they let only a few men know that the exalted Lord stands before them each morning upon awakening, holding His hand out to help them to find the answers to the troubles they will have to face during the day. The Father can help us by directing us to refrain from our negative spirit and our negative thoughts. With His help, we could regain enough of our original senses to endow us with hope and prosperity until the end of time. Man must understand how hard it is to reckon with *Truth Everlasting.* Man's hope is gone once he eludes the *Truths* that the Father placed into his memory bank.

Now, my child, this sermon is over. You have recorded a true event that took place down on the Earth centuries ago. You must teach men to abide with and live in the Lord's love and light and to seek a new beginning every morning of their lives.

HOW THE ANGELS TEACH US

In teaching men, we found the most difficult task was to teach them to care about one another and to take the teachings they had learned from the Father and Teachers and share them with others.

The Father wishes, above all else, that we love one another, care for one another and spread His teaching of *Truth* among all men. Each man was born to be a teacher of God's *Truths* and His *Laws*.

If we would greet the Lord each day of our lives, it would help rid us of all worry, hatred, and negativity. It would help us clear our minds, accelerate our thinking process, thus eradicating the negative clouds from our minds. It would help us to understand the mistakes that we make and often repeat so that we could cease to make them again. Furthermore, along this same pathway, the Father could re-teach us the *Truth* about our origin and why it is necessary for us to repeat some lifetimes over and over again. If we learn our lessons well when He stimulates our minds and deposits a thought, we will be able to repeat them to Him at a later time and this adds to His light as well as to our own. He would like to wipe away our fears. If He were able to do this, we could completely avoid any negativity that causes us to fear life in the first place. Negativity comes from man, not from the Father.

As we sleep and as we meditate, the Father is able to stimulate our thinking processes so that we can remember the lessons from the past which are pertinent to this lifetime. He tries so hard to teach man that there is a time to relax, a time to study—a time for everything. He wants us to take a vacation away from His teachings and studies, but when vacation time is finished, He expects us to respond to His teachings and start where we stopped before the vacation. He is determined to have us learn all the lessons that we came to learn in this lifetime. You see, my children, man can finish paying <u>his debt</u> in this lifetime and should strive to listen and learn so that he succeeds.

We who have been students of *Truth* have nothing to fear about *Life Everlasting* because we are constantly taught to rid our minds of fear and negativity about the hereafter. The efforts we put forth in learning God's *Laws* and lessons will see us in good stead and set us free to enjoy the life in the hereafter. The Father wants us to use the lessons we have been taught on a daily basis so as to refine our thinking. It is like practicing the piano every day until the notes flow in a beautiful fashion. He wants us to teach these lessons to any student who is willing to learn. Man should realize the fears that plague him--which occupies his mind—never truly existed. Man allows fear to stand in his way of perfection, allowing happiness, joy and peace to escape him.

The Lord loves us enough to keep us from hurt. We must all learn to understand this one statement. In order to enjoy

His love, all we have to do is renew our acquaintance with Him every day and set our minds free to accept all of His blessings, His love and His understanding. We must understand that He stands along side of us each morning to see how we are doing and to see if we, too, are planning to fulfill our mission and see how much we really love Him. He wants us to renew our faith on a daily basis. He then in turn renews His faith in us. Man must always remember that we cannot fool the Father because He senses and knows what we have in our hearts.

Whenever He wants us to live alone without His immediate guidance, which usually lasts only a short period of time, He warns our Masters and Teachers that they should watch over us. He knows beforehand what traumas and despairs we might encounter. He instructs our Teachers to help us as much as they can without directly injecting themselves into our lives and thus interfering in the lessons we must learn. He wants us to live our lives as independently as we can without asking for the aid of our Teachers for every want or need. The wise man on Earth knows that it is impossible to live alone for if the Father withdrew His light, we would cease to live. The wise man continues to believe in and trust the Lord because he knows that his expanse of consciousness and ideas come directly from the Lord's light. The Father wants us to live a healthy, happy life filled with light and knowledge of *Truth*. He wants us to enjoy our lifetime on the Earth.

In the beginning, before rebirth, we established a connection with Him that allows us to remember our mission on Earth. When He feels we are capable of listening and understanding, He is able to select the proper and precise thoughts to place into our memory bank. These are the thoughts that jog our memory and guide us to fulfill our mission keeping us on the right pathway. Occasionally man tires of these lessons and allows his free will to do as he pleases. The Father then allows us, your Teachers, to use other techniques that seem to allow us a little more freedom in helping man. If mankind sincerely wants to fulfill and finish all his obligations in this one lifetime, we allow him to appeal to us for help and direction and we do all that we are permitted to do. Man then must continue to greet the Lord each day with love and respect and continue to live life as was agreed upon before rebirth in a safe and happy manner.

Each man's mind contains the secrets of *Life Everlasting*; all he has to do is learn where the key is kept within his soul and unlock his memory bank in such a manner that he can express *Truth Everlasting*. Thus, if we find that inner "haven of refuge," we are on the road to finding the key to *Life Everlasting*.

THE TEACHERS SPEAK OF TRUTHS

As we have so often said, education can eliminate negative forces within man's mind, but not when man feels he is in charge of his life and obeys his own desires rather than that which he agreed upon with the Father. Occasionally, man can listen intently enough to be in touch with the Father. When this happens, he is determined to set aside time while living on the Earth to accommodate the Father's wishes because it brings comfort and happiness--a peace and harmony into his life that he had been seeking. Man forgets the original promises he made to the Lord. Man forgets that it is God Almighty, the Father of the Universe and the Brotherhood of Man, who allows us to live and function each day of our lives on the Earth. Today, exceptions are taken to the Lord's *Original Words of*

Truth. Man has his own interpretations and translations, but when adverse happenstance occurs within man's life thwarting his original purpose, he will try to recall one factor or part of his original promise. Man really does not care to recall his reason for living because then he would have to continue trying to fulfill his mission no matter how difficult it may seem. He involves himself in political and other life modalities on the Earth and allows them to take precedent over his original promises. Too often man does not leave enough time to adhere to the Lord's lessons on *Truth Everlasting*.

Man defers to the Father only during times of great upheavals and perils that involve his own life. At other times, nothing more matters to him than self-satisfaction and satisfying his own desires. Then it seems that *Truth Everlasting* is not important to him. If it were otherwise, man would choose to adhere to the rule of living closer to the Father's *Laws*. For instance, when one involves himself in dirty politics, what matters most at that time is being elected and nothing more. All other values fly out the window. Man obviously will use every method in the book to evolve and to achieve greater material wealth or self-gratification. Man must first learn his own true values by communing with the Lord each morning and asking for guidance and direction so as to follow one of the *Original Laws* which is "condemn no man." That is a viable way of life.

How soon will men recognize the *Truth* that, while mankind continues to wander aimlessly looking for purpose, his purpose was designated for him all along? Initially he understood his whole plan, but now he is thrashing around looking for and hoping to stumble upon his real purpose.

Man cannot overcome his fear of reality. It seems man fears for himself and his countrymen at this time in history more than all other times. In order to relinquish this fear, one must understand clearly the Father's lessons. The time is coming to the Earth when man will have to account for his actions and will have to know how to predispose his imaginary purpose. Mankind alone can create a holocaust; and as we continue to observe man's mind, it would seem to us a tragedy can be in the wings (that is, in the making). We see a certain faction from one area of the world-creating dilemma after dilemma to create chaos for mankind. As it comes more clearly into focus, the real purpose supposedly is to set the world afire with flames of propaganda but underneath it all is a commercial reason and counts for nothing more than the idolized almighty dollar. Otherwise, why is the current focus upon the oil countries? Commerce, money, and more commerce!! Why are the natives of certain African countries called upon to set fire to everything? It is for other governments to take over the country and gain more wealth, power and commerce.

We plead with the Lord each morning to try to hold back all injustices within men's minds. We proclaim freedom for all mankind rather than enslavement. The man who lives in the light, as students like you now teach, must learn to hold out a hand of wisdom to the wretched who are enslaved within their own minds. If we do not free man's mind from the personal enslavement that limits them in all ways of life, they become so embittered that they begin to teach hatred and failure and involve others who also feel enslaved. If this is allowed to continue, many will withdraw from society and truly feel enslaved without hope.

The Lord saith, *"Open thy minds to the beauty about thee and love thee one another."*

HOW TO GET RID OF POVERTY OF THE SOUL

We have been taught that all men were created equal, but no man is truly equal unless he <u>feels</u> he is and that he <u>can</u> be equal. Again the responsibility of life falls directly on our own shoulders. Equal opportunities afford themselves in every man's life. If man feels inadequate, the opportunity falls by the wayside. Man must re-evaluate himself before he blames society, family, and others--always looking for a copout for his discontentment. Please note that the word "failure" is not used because God does not see any of his children as failures. He only sees lost children who are not on their right pathway. If in our re-evaluation of lost opportunities, man is honest in his evaluation and realigns his thinking, there will be less loss of opportunities in his future.

Every man has an innovative spirit that wants to express *Truth*. We have always known *Truth,* but we repress our spirit in our daily lives because we feel our lives should always run smoothly and be perfect. If we try to excise all negative and mercenary thoughts, we can allow the Holy Grail to reveal itself. We should love ourselves and all of mankind, excluding <u>none</u>.

No matter how hard life becomes, there is adequate freedom of thought that can eradicate the negativity from the spirit of man. So surrender not to evil or negative men. Simply go about your daily lives living it to the fullest of your ability allowing the freedom of the spirit and soul to soar. Do not stray away beyond your beliefs into a world of unknown *Truths*. Man should enjoy his life and thus others will want to follow in his footsteps. They also want to share in the joy of living.

Accepting Negativity Into Our Lives

Destitute men and women who have programmed their lives ever to be destitute are as capable as any creature on Earth but by choice have chosen to fail. They program themselves for failure! Man must learn to distinguish truth from evil so that his thinking is wholly adjusted to accepting only *Truth.*

Each man possesses acute instincts that forewarn him of impending negativity trying to enter into his life. This instinct allows him a choice to select which way he wants his life to go. Accordingly we ask only for the opportunity to express, re-teach and stimulate the mind to the facts of *Truth* hidden within each man's mind. When a person in the educational system wants to express and impress an open mind with his "isms," it has been proven that the educator can teach the evil side to man. When evil thoughts are allowed to be placed into man's mind and he tolerates and allows them to seat themselves deeply into his subconscious it can affect his whole life in a negative way.

Ascertaining Truth

The same procedure can work with *Truth*. Education may stimulate *Truth* if only mankind allows it to filter down deeper into his subconscious. In this manner, man learns to evaluate good from evil (that is, *Truth* from evil) when it is presented to him. Unless man is viable and greets the Lord each morning, how can the Lord assemble and place *Truth*-giving guidance and direction into men's thinking? You see, my children, a deep, dark-kept secret allows man to understand His directions only if he allows the Father to communicate directly with him. The Father is allowed to teach and impress man's mind, thereby enabling man to assimilate *Truth* and to differentiate *Truth* from evil. Life then becomes easier to live when *Truth* and evil are sorted out, like separating the chaff from the wheat.

Current False Teachings

It is impossible to guess the amount of negativity that has been taught by so-called messengers of God, e.g. cults, teachers, and the television preaching of the supposed translating of *Truths*. These translations are not the complete *Truth*, but merely knowledge perverted into expressions that are used by these "preachers" for their own selfish purposes or goals. In His *Original Laws* or teachings, there is no word of discipline or judgment by man. Only God can truly judge man.

If a child is given love, discipline, and permission to be a normal human being and is allowed to make mistakes along the way, most often the child will not end up a victim. He learns from his mistakes and goes on to do better things and is less likely to be led into abject poverty of his soul by anyone. Now read on, my children, and see the comparison.

There is no given abject poverty level among man. Man creates this all by himself. There are truly no outside forces that can cause man to live beneath the poverty level if he is a healthy person. All of this is created by his own lack of motivation and elevation of spirit. He allows himself to live in such poverty because he is again without motivation, with no desire to educate the mind, and with futility contends that the "world owes me," or "I do not need to be responsible." These precepts which bring abject poverty to the soul and mind are created by man alone, not by God. Man can and should eliminate the master plan of his life that forces him to live in abject poverty. Man alone must eliminate all the negative excuses which allow him to blame everyone and everything for his discontent. He has the ability to reason away his difficulties if only he would look up and not just down and try to follow the Father's simple instructions of going the positive way of motivating himself. This can be done very easily by disciplining his mind to think about positive living to further himself. (Abject poverty would then be set at the minimum list in a man's mind rather than the maximum.) People who do not accept the God-given assortment of ideas and thoughts projected into their mind end up living in abject poverty of the soul, of the spirit, and of the pecuniary level.

ONE MAN DECIDED LIFE COULD BE EASIER
IF HE WERE AN INVALID
(A Parable)

As I sat down today to meditate, I immediately sensed a thought I had never considered. "Why would some men decide to return to Earth as invalids?"

Suddenly it was as though I were viewing a movie in color and sound; and as it began to unfold, I realized the person involved had a great dread and fear of living on the Earth caused by previous dismal lifetimes. He began to think, "If I could embark again on life's pathway by being an invalid or as a retarded individual, the Lord would help me along while I live on Earth; and my fellowmen would feel sorry for me and help me."

Daily he began to implore the Lord to allow him to be born as a disabled person. Some time went by, then suddenly one day, he found himself back on the Earth as a deformed individual.

It didn't take long before he realized his mistake--his life wasn't as he had envisioned it was going to be. He felt trapped in his body, always needing a certain amount of help from someone. He felt so alone and lonely all the time in this deformed body. He no longer thanked the Lord for sending him back deformed. Now he suddenly turned all of his anger against the populace--especially those who surrounded him every day. Then one day he decided it was the Father's fault even though he had implored the Lord to let him come back as a deformed person and the Father had answered his prayers. He began to feel the Father should have known better and should have saved him from this--his heartache.

Suddenly the picture changed and he was on the other side of the veil. One night he had just quietly passed on without anyone hearing his leaving. He then found himself facing the Lord; and as fond as he had been of the Father, he was afraid to face Him. He kept evading the meeting and would not look directly at the Father. He kept reminding himself of his own cowardly actions in different lifetimes. He knew if he faced the Lord, he would have to admit he was the one who made the original mistake and had falsely blamed the Father and his family.

As the time went by, he came face to face with the Father. He prostrated himself in the Lord's presence and began to beg, "Please forgive me Father. I meant You no harm when I condemned You for my misfortunes. True, I had asked You to send me back to Earth as a deformed man. I had concluded You would feel sorry for me and that with all of Your power and wisdom, You would help me function more like a normal man even with my frailties."

The Lord looked kindly upon this, His child, and answered, "When I refused to help you fake your way through your life, you decided to blame and hate Me. Does it not make sense to hate yourself first, then ask for forgiveness from your family and neighbors while you still lived down on the Earth rather than to whine and cry about your condition and blame everyone else?"

Thus saying these words, the Lord left him standing and wondering if ever the Lord would truly forgive him.

He began to work hard with the souls who were returning from Earth and tried to teach them all responsibility of self. He did not encounter the presence of the Lord until judgment was to be declared upon his request to return to Earth. As he appeared before the Lord, he began by saying, "Please forgive me Father; I shall reemerge as a healed soul down on the Earth. This time I am whole and willing to stand up to my responsibilities during my lifetime, if it is Thy will."

THE THREE LEVELS OF THINKING

There are three levels of thinking. Educate your mind to accept the thoughts only of the highest level. The first level is assigned to daily trials and tribulations; the second level recalls thoughts from past lifetimes; the third level accelerates our level of thinking from past lifetimes to help work out the present trials and other thoughts left to be explained about *Life Everlasting*. The third level can continue upward to the seventh level: A level which man should strive to attain before leaving the Earth. Mission completed!

Every morning man should begin with one single solitary thought that comes to his mind that needs to be addressed. This thought definitely should be finished before going about the day. We have been trying to help you select thoughts that have deep meaning for you so you will work harder on solutions and allow yourself to take on the responsibility of finishing that which you began long ago. Our responsibility to men is to bring forth the thought that we find lingering in their minds. We then accelerate their thinking and help them explore all avenues to retrieve all of the past unfinished responsibilities. Man should commence early each morning and digest this "food for thought" for it will help him raise his vibrations. If he will do this on a continual basis, it becomes a simple function.

It is much simpler to raise your vibrations to the highest level while living on the Earth. It becomes far more difficult after you pass to the next experience. In the next phase of living, there are several more levels of thought that we are not permitted to explain other than to say there are several additional levels to be accomplished. We beg all men to strive to elevate themselves several steps farther up the ladder of life now.

THE GATEWAY TO HEAVEN

The Masters say that it is important that mankind knows that there truly is a "Gateway to Heaven;" that it stands open to those of us to pass through freely, who are taking back adequate light and energy. What this means is that we have understood and live God's *Laws*, and taught them to others. Adequate light enables us to open the gate wider and pass more speedily through it.

The Teachers say that there are many men who have lived upon this Earth for centuries who refuse to learn anything else but what they learn this time on Earth, and they feel that is the real and only *Truth*. So these men will have to relive their lives until they accept the oft-repeated version that is brought to them in some way everyday by the Father. They cannot comprehend nor understand that the mercies that are showered upon them each day are the *Original Truths* they must learn before they can pass through Heaven's gate for all eternity. Indeed, many feel these *Truths* are sent to them only to make them more fearful. Each and every one of us holds the original secrets of the *Truths* as they were spoken and taught to us by the Father. They are deeply ingrained into our consciousness; and if we would but allow them to float forward into our conscious mind, we would have all the tools that we need to return safely back home.

We must learn my children, how to live as God wishes us to

live. This must occur before we can advance to the highest level of consciousness so to enter the Kingdom of Heaven. Man can revive and relearn these *Truths* if he would but sit down every morning and ask the Father for help. If he would but learn how to meditate correctly, the answers would be placed into his mind. It is important to remember that we all are a part of one another's lives and that we must share all the knowledge that we have gained. In other words, we are again reminded of the two questions we are asked upon our return home by the Father:

1. *What have you done with your life?*

2. *What have you done for My children?*

MEMORY FILE

The Masters and Teachers who come into our lives during this lifetime want to help further our education. We meet many former enemies and friends in each lifetime. We have total recall from previous lifetimes--deja vu. Apparently, certain instances are pulled from our memory bank, but we seldom recall the entire incident. It just seems that we get a kaleidoscopic view of a memory, but many of the accompanying incidences are left blank because they are too painful to remember. Why relive negative experiences?

Can you remember the very first impressive thought that was instilled into your mind? Can you still recall that thought, if for only a second? Could you remember that first thought if your mind were under duress to do so? "No." But a simple "no" is not the complete answer. We all have a computerized mind that retains the original thought that our Teachers have taught us over the centuries, but we are remiss; we do not include those first thoughts in our present-day repertoire of subjects to ponder upon. They are so deeply planted in our memory bank and are not given the priority they deserve thus they are not as quickly available for recall as those thoughts of more recent vintage. Instead, we suddenly stop our minds from recalling the regal thoughts as we once did. At one time we were told to remember all of these thoughts because they would prove to be important to us. If only we could recall for an instant just one original lesson, it would help us to remember all that followed. For instance, is it not true that once you remember one thought does it not follow like a chain reaction, one thought brings on another? So it is with your deeper memory banks.

The solution to this puzzle of "lost" thoughts remains in abeyance. If we could treat our memory bank as the rich depository for our inevitable eventide of our lives where we placed all of our acquired rich accumulation of thoughts, events and deeds, then we would and could recall all of the happy instances that occur during our present lifetime.

Since man is accustomed to forgetting the bad or negative thoughts, he basks in present-day comforts rather than reliving past discomfitures. We want to make sure you understand what we are saying. As an example: When a person loses her mate suddenly, she remembers only the happy times. The departed soul, who may have been a tyrant, suddenly becomes a saint in her mind.

A PROPHECY
WAR COMES ON THE SIXTEENTH

My dear child, the information we are bringing to you now will cause your heart to ache, but we feel in all fairness we should prepare you for the events of war again. We would rather bring thoughts of happiness to you, but we have committed ourselves to teaching you *Truth* and, therefore, feel we must tell you of the impending conflict. We ask that you continue to pray and to think thoughts of a peaceful co-existence on the Earth. We must find a manner in which all of mankind can live peacefully and co-exist, no matter race, creed or nationality. We must find this peace on the Earth if the Earth is to remain intact. Man must combine the energies of health and happiness to guarantee all mankind a healthy and happy coexistence not just for the few, but for all mankind all over the world.

As we speak, horrible things are finding their way into man's mind. The spiritual side of man's mind is telling him to explore other ways in order to find a peaceful solution to all the trials and tribulations going on on the Earth today, but there is no answer to our combined pleas. You see, my child, we co-exist only because the Father allows us to co-exist, but our free will can destroy us all.

One thing we want to make clear now for the record: We want it plainly understood so that all mankind will know that this holocaust is not of the Lord's making. We know you have been exposed to this before, but we continue to reiterate it again and again until man understands that the Father has nothing to do with this situation. The co-existence among men is allowed only by man himself. *"I do not wish to overstay My welcome,"* the "Father says, *"but I must stay the execution of My children."* He was able to stay their hands this morning but it will not be for long as we see it happening the afternoon the Sixteenth of January of the Lord's year 1991.

I am your Master Teacher and I wish to bring you this information. You must recall that the plans once laid out are planned to happen, often referred to as being "written on the wind." That plan will be worked out but perhaps differently than you had thought. But it will be worked out. Do not be afraid that man will be led to slaughter as soon as the planes fly. We see it beginning at night because the sorties will begin when the moon is not so full. The time element is so crucial, and they know they dare not delay too long for they have been warned of the changing of the weather.

The Almighty Father sits back watching from afar and waits for the infirm or dead to reach His state of consciousness.

Dear Reader:

This information was brought to your author just

before the Gulf war erupted and was related to a meditation class of ten people three days before the war started.

It was also predicted that the war would end too soon and would lead to other wars which could be settled now if the politicians would let the Generals run the war.

WHO CREATES WARS?

Dear child, we would like you to discard all of your woes and cares and be completely at peace so that we can speak with you this morning.

Let us begin with this thought: Equality among mankind as was originally taught by the Father was that each man was truly created equal and that we were each of us important in God's scheme of things.

We were taught to live each day as though it were the last day. Somehow, man looks upon his daily life now as a greasy grind, accepting thoughts of negativity rather than looking at life each day with great anticipation and as a challenge. If man would accept both good and bad as part of everyday living and allow his mind to balance out these conditions, he would soon see the Universal Law works for him just as it does for all of mankind. It is important for mental health to educate men's minds to accept what comes. When man does not accept his fate, like the daily greasy grind of just living upon the Earth he replaces the peace and harmony that he brought forth with him. Again we repeat that our original purpose--our mission to Earth--was to unite all men unto a common cause and that cause was to respect and love the Father as well as each other. Where today is the Father earnestly worshipped exactly as He was before man was placed on the Earth? Where among men today is there a similar situation about *Truth* and God's *Laws* in existence as they existed before our rebirth?

This is why you can say that He came to Earth among us to teach us again how to live all the *Truths* and the lessons for His way of life. He has sent us many great teachers--like Christ himself--to try to lead us back and teach us how to live and understand the *Truths Everlasting*. There is no doubt within our minds--those of us who live on the other side of the veil--that *Truth* will eventually win out over negativity, but times are now fraught with negative men and women who allow thoughts of negativity to remain in their minds. It has become a way of life. They never give a fleeting or second thought to *Truths*.

A Word of Warning

Now we are going to illustrate what we are talking about. We ask you to accept this word--this one word of warning. We offer you this word of warning because we know how much you love mankind and how you grieve for one who is hurt by injustice. Do not allow yourself to be overcome with grief for those men being slaughtered within the confines of their own homeland. Soon there will be a stop put to this evil man. It should never have been allowed and could have been stopped before, if only those who say they stand for freedom would have awakened. The wise men are being advised not to trust this tyrant, no matter what promises he makes to the world. My child, as we see him, he is useless garbage among men, but he has instilled the evil power into his hands and has taken over his land with an iron fist. We see how distraught you are for the innocent children, but do not worry. Someone will stop his advancement into other territories. It matters not what he says. He not only wanted Kuwait but Saudi Arabia as well, so that he could terrorize the whole world with his control over the oil supply and with his atomic bombs. That will not occur because the whole world will attack his country and he will be decimated within a month's time and many of these problems will be solved. Unfortunately, many new problems will occur as a result of this war. It is not the end but a preface for what is to come.

A new battle starts today. Men should reproach those involved in allowing this to happen because it could and should have been resolved before it got this far. It is as though the world wanted war. Remember when Israel tried to wipe out the manufacturing of chemicals. The whole world cursed her for what she did. Now they wish she had invaded the land of Iraq and sent this tyrant fleeing for cover. The war will not last more than a month or two at the very most. You will begin to see other countries bordering this madman start to see and understand his evil empire that he has instilled within his land and they will send troops for their own protection in order to survive. The tyrant will lose much and he will try to make offers to try to stop the action, but this could and should have been done before the war began.

We want these words recorded for mankind to know that this war has been a kind of fraud perpetuated upon mankind.

Work for Peace

Who starts all the wars? God does not!

Since the early beginning of time, the Father sought refuge for us from other men. He did not send us to the Earth to fight one another, but to solicit aid for one another and receive succor ourselves. We all needed to know this and to know how He felt about us. The entire world needs to know that He loves all of mankind and that He seeks peaceful solutions to all of mankind's problems.

Today among men there is a sort of pseudo-truce waiting for a holocaust to again happen. There is no current peaceful solution. Man's idea is to "shoot it out" or find a way to "stab a man in his back." These appear to be the only solutions man knows today.

According to this text, the Lord wishes for peace above all else. His solutions are understood today but they are hidden deeply in mankind's hearts and souls. Even so they are aware of His wishes, and of His preferences and opinions. Does man deem it a privilege to pray and meditate? It seems no is the answer unless some calamity happens to him.

Always Remember

Forgiveness of self is most important. Only then can God forgive us! Should we not forgive our fellowman his frailties? God does!

TRUTH EVERLASTING

The Masters return to the lengthy subject titled *"Truth Everlasting."*

I have often tried to impress upon your minds that the Lord loves us all. I know that is simply spoken, but please realize it is a far-reaching *Truth*. If only mankind could come to the realization that he is deeply loved by the Father, he would lose all fear of living.

The Father advises us on a daily basis on how to escort ourselves through this lifetime. Of course, happenstance occurs within every man's life. It is how we handle each happenstance, how we try to advise and help our fellow man to handle his happenstance that we are finally judged.

Man has to understand what happiness is so to be able to accept happiness when it comes to him. What we are saying is that unless you know what happiness feels like, how can you accept it or know about it? That is the challenge to mankind, to truly learn how to feel the different emotions that come into play during his lifetime. He must have feelings in his heart for mankind. First, he must feel mercy for if he does not have mercy within his heart for others, he will have to be taught the meaning of mercy. He must learn this, and often does, through many hardships while he lives on this Earth.

When a man begins to think only of his own joy--his own happiness--and thinks that his happenstance is worse for him than others, then he is in deep trouble because his ego could never accept an accident happening to him--doesn't it always happen to others? He is just unprepared and cannot handle adversity. He uses or wastes his light in protesting his fate. When the time comes for him to return to the Father, that person will stand before the Lord trying to explain his returning without sufficient light or energy so that his signal could be very easily identified.

This is a good lesson on *Truth Everlasting*. We wish every man on Earth would study it carefully and learn from it for no one escapes the process of living and returning.

We now wish to continue with the thought that man must learn to accept his fellowman for what he is and the way he is. If one could teach himself to accept this thought, it would eliminate the negative thinking and feelings directed toward his fellowman. In educating your mind in this fashion, you eliminate the negativity that gathers around you. Wisdom can help you to eliminate all negativity. Though we want you to live close to all of mankind, you need not hold on to those who insist upon living in their own negative way; you do not have to feel guilty if you do not hold them close to your heart. You need not live with negative people; but you cannot destroy their faith in you and your understanding of them. You do for them what you can, slowly weaning yourself away. Say to yourself, "Were it not for the hand and eyes of the Lord, there would go I." Feel sorry for the man who is negative. Think of the courage he must muster to face life alone. Have pity or mercy for him. When you sincerely worry and have pity upon your fellow man, the Lord blesses you and knows your true feelings.

The negative man who feels that he has been put upon hates the Earth and all of mankind because he feels he is totally alone in his suffering, thinking that no one else suffers but him. Another negative man vents his anger and often wishes he could leave the Earth. He will have to learn how to handle his anger alone. One can only suggest and guide such men, but one cannot do for them what they must do for themselves. These troubled individuals seem not to understand that as long as man has his health, he can truly handle whatever he has to face in this lifetime. Recall that we previously said: It is how man handles happenstance that really matters.

As long as we face life frontally, cognizant that others suffer also, then we shall stop feeling sorry for our own heartaches and we shall never feel alone. It does not matter how much solace we might feel for mankind in his troubled state. All we can do is try to guide him to help himself. Say: "I will help you; I will try to soothe you; but in the final instance, you alone can help yourself."

THE MIGHTY OAK

(A Parable)

On the morning of April 24, 1984, I knew I was going to receive something very beautiful and profound. I felt the presence of two of my Master Teachers. Almost immediately I began to see pictures of a hurricane in action. A huge oak tree was also shown to me, bent over, almost touching the ground. Instantly, it seemed that all of the leaves were blown from the tree and as I watched, it seemed to me a miracle was taking place for as soon as the buffeting winds had subsided, the mighty oak raised her beautiful head and stood proudly erect. The Masters said to me:

"You see, the oak tree is still alive and as strong as ever. She remembered her consciousness. She knew how to bend to avoid disaster."

Additionally, the Earth also benefited from the leaves and used them as a fertilizer to renew itself, thus making the Earth grow in size and it was then ready to be used for planting and harvesting. Because the tree bent, it did not break or die. So man should react when the hurricane or holocaust strikes in his life. Man should be prepared, as was the mighty oak, with lessons etched in awareness as how to react to the holocaust. The Masters spoke, saying:

"Now that you have seen this picture, we wish to further elucidate upon it: You saw a mighty oak tree standing firm and straight. Yet, when the hurricane ripped through, it happily shed its leaves to protect its strength and thus added energy to the Earth, helping in the renewal of the soil so that the Earth was prepared for sowing and reaping. During all of the time that the hurricane continued, the mighty oak tree was bent over and remained so until it knew the wind had subsided. Then miracle upon miracle, the mighty oak stood straight once more, ready to re-grow new leaves and allow the peaceful breezes to again playfully rustle its leaves and the birds could nest safely within its branches, and its fruits would sustain many more of God's creatures.

"If you were watching closely as the wind bent the tree, you remember that the oak did not break because it held firm onto its consciousness. So, my child, it should be with men. They should learn to sort out facts of substance--know what is reality and what is fantasy.

"We have taught you for a long time that this life is a fantasy and the next phase of living is reality. Each person is encouraged to express desires, hopes and wishes. He may also have any unanswered questions brought to fruition through visualization and meditations. When this occurs, man releases energy into the atmosphere and just as the oak provides fertilizer (or energy) to the soil, so man provides energy by using his mind correctly. Man should be encouraged to voice or in some way release his thoughts or ideas into the air so that he shares his energies to sustain all (as the oak leaves sustained many). When the hurricanes or any adverse happenstance occurs in his lifetime, he should learn how to bend. He should not be so foolhardy as to stand erect defying a mighty hurricane; defiance, a combative attitude, creates negative energies. Again and again, this released energy resulting from a peaceful consciousness is needed to preserve his lifetime on Earth. Therefore, learn to wait for disastrous winds to subside before resuming life in a normal manner. It is as simple as that."

Another interesting illustration was brought forth on

this particular morning. The example was the washing machine.

The Teachers began with this comment, "If dirt is embedded in your soiled clothing, would you not pre-treat or soak them to dissolve and to loosen the dirt from the fabric? Do you not help the washing machine then get rid of the dirt completely?" This analogy coincides with life on this Earth as follows: Pre-treat your fellow man's troubled spirit by presenting ways he can rekindle his faith in himself--help him solve his problems himself. Do not do it alone for him. This follows the mighty oak's example also, which illustrated that you are to shed your leaves as you can (that is, your wise counsel) to nourish the seedbeds of others, but leave the harvest to them.

Do not attempt to solve another's troubles for him or her. You can only resolve your own problems; that helps you to fulfill your destiny as it was meant for you to do. Stray not from your original purpose or the *Original Laws* you have learned. When the hurricane takes place in your lifetime on this Earth, you must learn to bend and accept the lessons learnt from the experience, but once again we remind you not to take on another's hurricane until man faces the experience and has regained his composure.

HAVEN OF REFUGE

Today is a beautiful day--if only man would look up instead of looking down! Listen to the wind. Today it is playing a beautiful song that can be interpreted as music by those who have the ear to listen.

Listen to the bird. He, too, is singing a different song as each bird was given a different song to sing for man's pleasure. Since God is the Master of all living things, so He is the Master of the wind and the birds.

There is a place in every man's mind called a *"haven of refuge."* Man must learn how to locate that haven in order to sustain himself through periods of turmoil in his life. Man must take God in as a partner and school himself to greet the Father each morning upon awakening with love and blessings in his heart and a song in his soul. In this way, he opens his mind to allow the Father to direct him and teach him the lessons he must know that will enable him to live that very day. As he blesses and listens to the Father, he is repaying the Father for all of the grace and blessings he receives daily. Showing an expression of his love and respect for the Father is one way of locating that *"haven of refuge."* Another is through daily meditation and prayer. The *"haven of refuge"* helps man focus on his pathway, but each man has the responsibility of finding it. As we mentioned before, man can use it in time of upheaval, unhappiness and other unforeseen traumas. When man finds his *"haven of refuge,"* he is rewarded with peace, calm, harmony, love, and answers to counter his traumas.

If man desires to live life to its fullest, he must discover the meaning of *Life Everlasting* and learn how to discard negativity before it roots itself within his mind. The *Giver of Truth* asks only that you live your life as His helper--as a *Giver of Truth* for His children--that you be able to extract from the lessons learnt yesterday those things necessary to help you to live today. Man must learn to extract from previous lives only the positive lessons--the *Truths* needed to help him to succeed today--thus helping him find his way out of the maze called "life." When we learn how to find our way out of the maze, it will lead us directly to the top of the mountain which is called the *"Top of God's Crest,"* known as *Truth Everlasting.* The first and most important thing to understand is how to extract himself from negativity by saying, "I will not accept a negative thought. I shall discard those thoughts that fight to overcome my thoughts of good."

When there has been a man true to God, as many of you have been in past lifetimes, He rewards him in this lifetime by asserting His positive will upon his mind, helping him to find happiness and joy which man has always searched for in his previous lives. Now, this is a *Truth:* It has been discovered that each man prophecies his own future before rebirth in that which he chooses to bring about in this lifetime--called his purpose or mission on Earth. He ordains these things for himself. Thus his reward is exactly as he has chosen. If man asks to be excused from fulfilling his purpose, when he returns home, it will bring severe criticism from his brethren, on the other side of the veil, who have tried to help him fulfill his mission while he lived on the Earth. Thus man should feel obliged to fulfill that which he chose to do on Earth so that all his Masters and Teachers can also be fulfilled. That essentially is what this lesson is all about. Do not defer to others. Say, "I shall remain alive and happy for as long as the Lord wishes me to live, and I shall fulfill each day in the manner that He commands me to do."

Man must understand that he must live one day at a time. That is true, but he also has to think a bit about tomorrow. In other words, thoughts like this mean we have to advance and use our minds. We must project our minds into the unknown and pick up an inkling of what is about to happen. We all have the ability to do this, but few wish to extend their minds further out into the ether. Negativity lurks constantly in every man's mind, but it can be overcome by being persistent in replacing the negativity with thoughts of *Truth*. Negativity robs men of the ability to succeed.

The reason the Father returns to teach us is to prepare us to face *Life Everlasting*. We must remember that there is not one *Master of Truth* who has not first fulfilled his destiny while living down on the Earth. The Father, as was originally mentioned, also comes back when we bless Him with our love and attention. He comes back to help us find that *'haven of refuge"* that can be found within every man's mind. Do not be afraid to call to Him for help.

MAN'S MISSION IN LIFE

Good morning, my child.. As we greet you this morning, we have a word of complaint for all mankind. Why do men not take the time occasionally to completely think through one thought? We feel it is because mankind avoids deep or serious thinking. We feel stymied and do not know how to help man when we are not allotted enough time through meditation or quiet time to educate man's mind. A sense of reclusiveness comes into being when we are denied the time. Then we ask, "How hard is it for men to plan a particular time each day to see us? We who are trying so hard to help you cannot understand why we are denied the time to help you become people of wisdom. Without wisdom, how can you hope to attain your highest state of consciousness or to survive in your competitive world?"

I will remind you again that "time immemorial" is a positive and definite thing that continues on into infinity. My child, man allows his precious time to escape from him that allows him to enjoy knowledge and wisdom.

Your guides sense a new time coming into mankind's lives. It is a time of change. Man will educate his mind and his psyche to accept the changes, but when the changes occur, he will finally resign himself to accepting the *Truth* that life immemorial continues on into infinity. Lest we forget the Master's original thought, they continually remind us that the Father wished us to remain alive on the Earth while we are productive among men; but when the time came, we felt alone, aimless and without purpose in this lifetime. It was then the time--if it is God's will--to relieve ourselves of the burden of living alone on the Earth.

This ties in with our *Original Teachings* that we were taught by the Father in the beginning of time--that when the original outline or covenant for each person's life was completed, we had in the beginning also agreed on the time of our death. So, after our productive period of life, our higher consciousness would instruct us that the time of death was near.

Thus man must pray each day that he has fulfilled his original mission--his covenant--otherwise, not only has he failed himself but all of the Masters and Teachers who have attached themselves from the very beginning to help him through this period of life on the Earth. According to this line of thinking, the Father accuses us all of reneging on our purpose during our time spent on the Earth. In other words, we deter ourselves from actually having any true meaning of purpose in this lifetime--which includes all of us who have lived before as well as those who will follow. As of today, we have all chosen the path of least resistance. We must not allow that to continue to happen because for mankind to take the easy way out once he understands his goals in this lifetime is simply asking to be returned to Earth to live again and again. Our mission only becomes more difficult each time we return until we fulfill our mission. Man must understand how hard it is to follow his instincts and teachings, but he should not capitulate so easily by giving up on himself or by accepting someone else's solutions.

Man must organize himself while he lives on the Earth and schedule enough time to acknowledge the presence of his Teachers. He should allow time to meditate and allow them to help enlighten him. It is important for us to learn our reason for being on Earth and that is to be able to take God in as our partner each day. We must learn how to show our appreciation for His efforts in our behalf and to acknowledge our divine and loving teacher. It is the truly greatest part of our mission. When we accomplish this feat, we should--without hesitation--continually send out our thoughts and expression that we have learnt about the Father into the universe so all can benefit. It helps us to understand part of our mission down on the Earth. We are acknowledging His existence. We are blessing Him for the grace and the love that He has given to us each day of our lives. In repayment for all His energy, love and grace which He has generously bestowed upon us, we must help spread His wisdom over the entire universe. If we fail in this mission at this time in history, evil will take over and be worshiped in place of the Father. Just look at the amount of Satan worship in the world today! Men will then understand why it is so urgent that man live close to the Father and set the example for His family and fellow men.

The world is going through an important change; and while

we live to see it happen, we will accept no excuses as to why we have failed to support the Lord in His wisdom and His teachings. We simply _must_ grow in consciousness; we must gather our own energy to a height that no man could endow us with more. With more energy and wisdom, we are led to learning to master the real _Truths_. We do know that education alone stimulates the mind, but wisdom comes only to those men who seek after wisdom the hard way. You must remember, my child, that the energy level of mankind differs from person to person. We cannot expect the same consciousness level in each man. When we face opposite poles of thinking, we herald a new beginning for it stimulates mankind into thinking and reasoning.

Why do we stress education so much, you may ask? We have learned that education does dispel and delete negative thoughts and that wisdom comes only to the man who is willing to set his mind free to soar into the outer perimeters of the universe so that when it returns, the mind is filled with wisdom. Thus, you see, he has learned through his adventures of _Life Everlasting_. _Truth_ becomes wisdom only when _Truth_ is truly understood. My child, this is the most difficult point to get across to man. The reason for that is due to the fact that the evil spirit within man occasionally says, "No, don't expend the energy to allow your mind to go out into the universe. Let me show you an <u>easier</u> way to reach the higher roads, but do not try to do it alone. Let me help you." <u>Do not accept this simple solution</u>. As they say: when something looks too good to be true, it probably is too good to be true, indeed. Nothing comes the easy way. You must halt the attempt by any negative force to lead you astray.

We would like to leave you with this thought: It is simple arithmetic if you accost evil or negativity over and over again, you use subtraction; and if you manifest the *Truth* each time you eliminate the negative--thereby allowing *Truth* to rule supreme--you are using addition.

To those of you who read this lesson, we ask that you do not discount one word of the wisdom that we have brought to you this day. Delete not one idea. Try to work it out in your mind so that you understand it completely and speak the wisdom contained therein; the Lord shall truly bless you.

FREE WILL

MEN HAVE MULTIPLE CHOICES IN LIFE

When I sat down at the typewriter this morning, immediately I heard Enoch say to me, *"Look me up in the Old Testament. I am a patriarch, I was the father of Methuselah who lived 969 years, and I am the son of Cain."* It was difficult for me to then concentrate on what he was about to relate to me. He began:

I am Enoch, the Prophet of *Truth*. I would wish to share these few words so that you understand how important it is to speak the *Truth* when explaining the way of life. Do not try to emboss or gloss over it to make man more comfortable, for *Truth* is exactly the way it is. Not all that is taught today to man is *Truth*, but man can feel when something is told to him, whether he can accept it as a matter of fact or fantasy. Do not find excuses for any man if he attempts to distort the Lord's word. I wish you to frame this thought into your mind. Distort not the meaning of these words. In the recesses of man's mind can be found many of the past *Truths*, but man avoids that today because he feels the subject is too profound for him to try to understand.

Our hope is that later in this lifetime, we will be able to lift those *Truths* from the recesses, for they will set man free. When these *Truths* are revealed, it will set the world aflame because they have long been forgotten. You must teach man that the access to these *Truths* remains available to all. All he has to do is search his own memory. Even his dreams represent something more than just a dream that allows his mind to rest. Dreams try to bring forth a subject to stimulate a thought for man to commence working or thinking upon.

Try to understand that mankind has multiple choices in this lifetime. He must determine which selections suit him best. Not all men are cut from the same piece of fabric; not all men are alike. We are proposing that all men have choices, and he must select the one that he feels most comfortable with. Spiritual education helps man transport these choices of thoughts into the unknown crevices within man's mind. You see, mankind hunts constantly for solutions during his entire life but all the time he is hunting out there, the solutions are buried within his mind.

Education in *Truth* primarily helps one to shuffle and discard thoughts that have little meaning. What I am saying is that it can help you exploit the truthful thoughts and discard the erroneous ones. Education helps to sort out *Truth* from evil--like the wheat from the chaff. Secondly, we wish to reiterate and make very clear that man sorts these thoughts alone. His selection depends upon himself and him alone. Therefore, the majesty of *Truth* rests with him because it has been instilled within his own mind. If he rejects *Truth*, his spiritual education will be limited and this leads to many pitfalls in time to come. If he selects the right *Truths* and educates his mind to accept them and live by them, then his progress will be unlimited.

According to the scholars who gather in our midst, we salute the Lord each morning; we command Him to send *Truth* to us.

"Almighty Father of the Universe, help us select the right thoughts for our minds to absorb. Let us envision Truths only so that we might conduct our lives in the rightful manner. Amen."

Yes, everything is in our own hands. Our own free will

imposes sentences upon us if we do not select the correct *Truths* to live by. God bless all of you.

MAN CAN BE FREE

This morning you were awakened by hearing us repeat this prayer:

"Take me safely back home to Thee, O Father. Let my heart feel Your love, let my mind join with Your thinking, and let my lips speak only those words that You have taught me. Please lead me safely back home to Thee.

Amen."

Now think about these words and repeat them as often as you mind will allow. You will, as all men find, great peace and comfort in them.

Life continues throughout all eternity. This is a *Truth* that you have often heard repeated, but it is one thought that man seems to store away and is then forgotten by him. If mankind would exercise his mind, thus setting himself free, he could truly have a joyous life and be a joy to all of mankind. Many men feel as though they are prisoners while they live on Earth. They do not seem to remember that it was their choice to return.

We often speak about the exchange of energy among men.

No man can continually live alone because his disposition necessitates recharging his energy by communicating with others. When he communicates, thus having an exchange of energy, he becomes charged with electricity, regardless of one's color, race or creed. Actually, man is free from the very beginning; but it is man's mind that imprisons him and many, unfortunately, continue to feel their bondage all the years of their lives. If man would but take advantage of all the possibilities that surround him and allow freedom to come into his thinking, he would then realize that he has, within his own mind, all the answers, all of the capabilities that he would ever need to live as a free man.

Man needs to receive the energy that he can get by communicating with his fellowman; then he can enjoy *Truth Everlasting* because then it becomes a simple process. Acceptance of life is important, but more important is the acceptance of the *Truth* within one's own consciousness or mind. Man learns to excel in life through acceptance of this *Truth*. In this way, man accepts only the positive way of living which follows a cycle certain to expand his consciousness and thinking so that he lives a truthful life. Man must continue to live with hope in his heart. Faith brings hope.

It has been suggested that we try to conjure up the appearance of His face as often as possible and think about His words as we meditate and pray. Acceptance of His light is not enough to ensure contentment in our lives. We must continue to search for wisdom, combining and allowing our faculties to be used in this search for *Truth*. The Almighty Father's wisdom of the ages belongs not only to us but also to the whole of the universe. Show us a man who is distraught with fear, and we will show you a man who has lost his faith in God and himself and has completely lost his sense of direction. The way to clear up his mind and set him on the straight pathway again is not to condemn him, but rather to set him free again, saying to him, "Look for the stars to guide you. Look for the *Universal Laws* to teach you to bring back the light and peace into your mind. Set your mind free. You do not live in bondage. Set your mind free of hatred and wanton thoughts."

Repeat this prayer,

"Please give me back my direction to the Laws of the Universe. Set me free again to understand Thy ways and thoughts.   *Amen."*

Each man must continue to practice and to learn new ways of expressing himself. Soon he will find himself in tune with mankind as well as with the Father. It is so important for man to be at peace with himself and to place his foot upon the pathway that will lead him back home. The end of life's trail comes upon us too quickly. We had better be about our Father's business together for, remember, man cannot live alone.

PART III

THERE IS RELIEF FOR THE BELIEVER
THE WORD OF GOD

One of the more important lessons mankind came to learn was patience; in conjunction with that, man needs to relearn the *Truths* that were taught to all many centuries ago. We must above all have faith and confidence in those *Laws* as well as in the teachers, guides and healers who guide us. They can teach us the lessons, they can offer directions, but they are not permitted to interfere in our lives. Our guides are not just teaching us for a specific moment in time but rather for what we call "tomorrow," which is in reality "forever."

We here know that the "Lord" brought us the *"Laws of God."* We are His sheep and He continues to be the shepherd over all of mankind, for God is *Love,* God is *Truth,* God is the light or the power or energy that makes us who we are. When man truly perfects his faith in God, he has no fear, no doubts, nor does he ever lack confidence in any situation. In the 23rd Psalm that you read before class each week, you repeat the following: *"Yea, though I walk through the valley of the shadow of death, I shall fear no evil."* Can you explain why you feel no fear? *"For Thou art with me and Thy rod and Thy staff comfort me."* We here refer to the rod as a rod of *Truth* and the understanding is the staff. To paraphrase: The staff is the understanding which gives to us the courage to face life. So knowing this, why do men still hold on to fear? Isn't the answer evident? It is because our faith is not strong enough, because we do not apply or live the *Laws* we have been taught each day. My children, each morning redefine your beliefs, your goals and your faith.

Man's Responsibility of Right and Conscientious Living

As your tapestry of life is woven each day of your life, keep this thought in mind: You still have to fight to overcome much from your past lives to be able to concentrate daily on weaving your daily portion of your life's pattern. Living right and conscientiously allows us to weave our tapestry through our daily living. You must do your best at sending out thoughts of love continually from your heart for all of God's children, and you will find your tapestry growing in pattern, and thus your love of God grows even stronger. If we live with *"love"* the way the Father taught us, we cannot help but fulfill that which we came back to re-weave on our tapestry.

Remember, my children, that thoughts become things. Caution your mind and be wary of what you wish for or think about for yourself as well as for all of mankind. The *Laws* are irrefutable: Negativity begets negativity. Good begets good.

GOD IS LOVE

On this particular morning as I sat to begin my meditation, a beautiful rainbow of light appeared, followed by a beautiful face surrounded by the whitest light that mankind could ever imagine. The following lesson from my beloved Angel Teacher flowed forth:

"In this lifetime on Earth, we must learn to accentuate positive thoughts and disregard negativity. In this lifetime, man must learn to stay with the positive thoughts or he will succumb to fantasy forever."*

22*NOTE: In our book, How to Find Your Way Back Home, our present earthly life is called "fantasy" and the next phase or spiritual life is called "reality." In other words, "reality" refers to the spiritual life or the next phase of living; "fantasy" equals our present life on Earth.

This morning the Teachers explained, "You have seen the pathway that was shown to reveal the Lord's face. It was brought very close to you, displaying the shower of light that lives around Him. He questions whether you attract as much attention to His work as you should be attracting by telling mankind, Remember: Infinite wisdom comes to those who believe in the Lord's light and *Laws*."

Accuse No Man

Accuse no man of harboring any ill feelings toward you or yours. Always say, "I feel kindly toward all men, and I wish they too would feel the same." The Lord salutes us each morning when He reinserts our light. He wishes us well in our daily lives. He has grown accustomed to seeing us fall, falter and relinquish control over our lives to others. This manner of demise among mankind elucidates man's own thinking and helps him to accept this type of role during this lifetime. If he had not faltered nor slipped into his lethargic feeling about life, he could still be holding his head high and working toward fulfilling his mission on Earth. The Father's advice is never to relinquish control of one's life to any man. Say to him, "The Lord bestowed His power of thinking upon me. He is August and Supreme in His thinking. He fears for no man as long as man can hold his head high, has faith both in the Lord and himself and condemns no man."

The reverse psychology works fine in most cases but by using your life as an illustration to those around you, you can teach them about fair treatment by the way you treat all men. They in turn will fear for the worst if they treat you or others unfairly. You see, you turn their distrust into respect.

The demise of mankind comes about when he slumbers along life's pathway sleeping during the daytimes of his life. Instead of recalling and reliving past lifetimes, let man learn to live in the present. This moment is all that is promised. Man must send out love to all who hate him or distrust him. In sending out thoughts of love, he must understand that he is forever relinquishing those thought waves of hatred that he feels for man; that he is then entrusting his lifetime on Earth into God's hands. The love he expends will come back tenfold if he is sincere in letting go of all hatred.

You recall God's admonition to us when He released us upon the Earth: He saluted us each morning with thoughts of great wisdom, saying:

"Use your light correctly and do not fear life. You came back to Earth in this lifetime to prove this point: Love can conquer all. Love yourself and all your fellowmen. Just give out vibrations of love."

Defame No Man

Say, "I have heard about so and so, but I fear I do not understand this man's thinking. If it is true and he has treated you in this fashion, I cannot understand a man's treating anyone thusly. It is hard for me to reconcile my thinking with a beast like that." You see, you excuse yourself from defaming any man, you educate your audience to see that you do not dislike any man, you are only repeating what you have heard. Thus, you avoid creating more karma for yourself during this lifetime.

In this dimension, seek and ye shall find happiness, health and all good things. Educate your mind to accept only good thoughts. Acquaint yourself with happiness--not despair; with health--not illness; and with love--not hatred; and enjoy your lifetime on this Earth. Indeed, this lifetime as are all lifetimes on Earth, a very short visit.

When we salute the Lord each morning, we insult Him by asking, "Can You help me live my life?" We knew in advance what we had to face while living on the Earth. Why insult Him by saying, "Come into my life and make the picture clear for me so that my life can be easy?" It would suddenly seem that you have forgotten your responsibilities. See what we mean?

Accept your life; work it out the best way you can. Afford Him the privilege of seeing how hard you have worked at making your lifetime a success. Consult with Him and ask for His advice only when you have finished doing the job as best you can. We want you to understand that this is not a contradiction. You know beforehand what you have agreed to do. Each morning we only ask for guidance and direction. Then when we have gone as far as we can in a situation and can then go no further, we do not just throw up our hands in disgust; it is then that we ask the Lord for help and we relinquish the situation into His hands. It is surprising how effective this relinquishing can become if we truly put it into His hands and allow our minds to be free to accept His answers. You have performed thus far most adequately, but the future holds many traumas for us all. It is how we face those traumas that will count in the future as to how we will be judged when we return safely back home to our Father.

Salute the Lord each morning asking Him only for advice and to give you the necessary light, energy, and knowledge to fulfill this day. Do not implore Him to live your life on Earth for you, but only to advise you how to live each moment the best way possible. You might use the following thoughts and words:

> *"Regardless of how difficult my life becomes, I only want Your ideas, Your guidance, and Your advice. I shall try to live this life You have given to me to the best of my knowledge and ability."*

This is all we may say to you this morning. We wish you a good day.

EXTOL MANKIND

This is the beginning of a subject that we will continue to bring to you from time to time that we wish you to record for posterity. It is a very simple thought: "Extol all of mankind."

We wish to help eliminate the negativity found within your

minds. Teach them that by saluting the Lord each morning, we add to our own lives and light. It helps us to accumulate more light, so as to extend our lives, whenever we come in contact with the Lord's light. We are trying to teach man that he can create things through his own thoughts. He must learn to expound upon justice and mercy. If he bars hatred and negativity from his own mind, learning to extol the Father, help will be sent to him to find the divine pathway—bear in mind, by extolling all men, we are in turn extolling the Holy Father. A daily prayer that should be used as we prepare for bed in the evening is as follows:

> *"Holy Father, help us all find the pathway that leads easily back home to Thee and protect my soul through the night.*   *Amen."*

Today we are reminded of a time when the multitudes of men sought after the Father; but once they found Him, they ingested His thoughts and then they allowed them to lie dormant in their minds for centuries. *Use the words of Truth each day of your life.*

We hope and pray for those of you who read these lessons and these words of *Truth* that you will use them each day of your life and that these words will act as beacons and signposts for man to find his way safely back to shore.

OUR SIGNAL

Always greet and welcome us with your smile and laughter. In so doing you are able to leave fear in the background.

No man should fear the Lord just because He is ever in attendance. He is trying to educate us. That is the purpose of this lifetime; it is a school to teach man how to live with one another. He loves each of His children in the same manner and He wants all of His children to love one another.

We were reincarnated for a reason. We are often asked how the Lord can tell one of His children from another. The answer is by "your signal." Now, what is the signal, you may ask. Look at your fingerprints. Do you notice that your fingerprints are different from your neighbor's and that there are no two sets of fingerprints that are exactly alike? So it is, my children, with your signal. Your light shines brightly or dimly, depending upon how much energy you have accumulated through your learning processes. In this way the Father always knows where each of His children is located. Since energy never dies, and that fact is common knowledge among your scientists, that thought leads us to accept and believe that the energy called mankind continues to live forever, throughout all eternity.

When we are reincarnated, we live on the Earth our allotted years, but we do not cease to exist after that time. We simply go on to another phase of learning and living. The Father, who is our constant Teacher, leads us by His will, wanting us to succeed. You must understand that He uses our light wisely, but the light originally stems from His source. It is through this supply of His light that causes us to exist on the Earth at all. Without His light, without his wisdom, we would be lost souls wandering in the desert. This may seem to be a simplistic explanation of *Truth,* but it is a *Truth* just the same, for *Truth* is very simple. It is we, the Earthlings, who want to make it more complicated.

The Father is very kind, loving and understanding. He allows us to envision our lives down on the Earth as a successful adventure. Otherwise, we would not be allowed to reunite with Him in the end for we would consider ourselves unworthy. The Father blessed us by colonizing us, so to speak, by giving us our light to help us advance during our Earthly life. Thus in our gathering closely together, there is a tremendous exchange of energy and learning which helps us to enlarge and enhance our amount of light. We must remember if He refused us our use of His light, it would cause us to die instantly. Therefore, the fellow who has the ability to understand how to signal the Lord, that it is past his time to live on the Earth, can cause his fuse of light to burn brightly. It causes the Lord to notice that the man wants and needs to return safely back home. If a man deters from following through and living his life as he was taught, his fuse then becomes shorter and diminishes in strength. He does not feel life is worthwhile; therefore, his signal would be dimmer. That is what happens when a man commits suicide.

Therefore, we must live each day completely, living the *Laws* as they have been taught, reaching out to those who are in need and blessing the Lord each day, each moment of our lives. We must illuminate our minds with light created by His teachings, thus creating the fuse that will burn brightly--that will take us safely back home.

We want you to investigate this thought further. We want you to ask questions of yourself and of your Teacher. We want you to examine this one thing: The *hermit*. If every person lived alone, there would be no exchange of energy, so who would learn the *Truths*? Who else would teach about the Lord's light? Who would leave these words of wisdom for future generations? Do you understand, each of you, that without these lessons and messages of *Truth Everlasting* that no man on Earth would understand how hard it would be for him to reunite with the Father? That is why we are constantly reminded that we were meant to live in tribes, to share our energy, knowledge, etc. and never to live alone.

You must instill this thought into your mind: *"You must allow your light to glow brightly after you have lived your life. Then you must follow the light without fail into your next adventure."*

We are asked this question over and over throughout the centuries: What happens to man once he ceases to exist upon the Earth? We are delighted today that we have been able to come into focus with your Teacher's mind, allowing us to deliver this fuel for your learning apparatus. If you continue to allow your mind to be refueled during your lifetime on Earth, it will pay off when the time comes for man to repay the Father for this expensive journey.

It is by this refueling that the mind's eye is kept ignited and the trip taking us back to the Father is set straight and sure. If our demise should come "at an interim time" before the brain is thoroughly refueled our mission fulfilled, we must ask to live longer on Earth to regain our identity. By this we mean that the soul goes back to a lesser conscious level than when it entered the Earth; therefore, it will have to reincarnate again and again until the consciousness is refueled to its highest level—only then do we regain our identity.

It is our light--our signal--that sets us apart. Be sure, and be determined, to learn the lessons that you have to learn so as to add to your light and finish your mission. Do not allow anyone to hamper your understanding of your purpose. You shall then return at the allotted time, and you will then go directly to the Father.

REMEMBER YOUR SIGNAL

The Lord, blessed be His Name, made us aware of His presence long, long ago. He instructed us how to think very deep thoughts and how to plant them in the depths of our minds, thinking surely we would always remember these words of wisdom. The Father assigned to each of us a signal, so to speak, so that He would know exactly where we were and thus He could distinguish us one from another. After He set us free upon the Earth allowing us free will, the signal promptly left our minds. Try as we might, we could not find the words that had been recorded in our minds. We could not remember His teachings even though He had patiently given them to us over and over. Thus, we stumbled aimlessly along life's pathway, hoping and waiting for a miracle to occur. We hoped that He would return and re-teach us the lessons and our signal.

One day while we were trying to retrace our steps to where He had left us originally, we suddenly saw Him from afar. He was waiting for us, sitting on the stone that He had described to us as a meeting place. He had told us that we could always find Him waiting to teach and talk with us at this particular meeting site. We were so happy to see Him that we all ran to Him like little children, but His greeting to us was, *"Why have you not contacted Me before?"* Not one of us could find an answer without failing to tell Him the *Truth*. As I spoke, I told Him we had forgotten the signal that He had assigned to us and I implored Him by saying, "Dear Father, forgive us for this oversight; help us again." The Lord Over All of Us looked down into our faces for He was an August Person and said:

"I cannot talk with you any longer if all you can remember is the site of the rock. You can no longer see My face, and thus without the correct words to guide and direct your lives on a daily basis, you can no longer communicate through your light. Thus you have lost touch with Me completely."

The Father liberally dispersed thoughts of wisdom into our minds. They were simple thoughts used to express His concern for man. He relegated authority to us and made us responsible for remembering the many thoughts that He had given to us. He also cautioned us that it would be useless to remember His teachings if we did not use them. He instructed and advised that we would be in an enviable position on Earth if we understood and used the exact thoughts, for the Lord knew that few men would remember. Apparently, education fluctuates within each man's mind thus differing from man to man as to how he grasps, assimilates or understands the individual thoughts or quotations that sometimes are difficult to understand.

To understand man's attitude toward life is even more difficult than understanding his thinking.

A certain novice once directed me in this manner, "Commence to think like the Lord asked us to think. Evolve to the higher realm of thinking." You can do this by using the simple admonition He left with us when He placed us on this mainland:

"Use your heads, remember My teachings, remember all of the thoughts that I have sent unto thee, remember Me in holy places as well as in the lower forms of life for, remember, that I am in all you touch and in all that you see; and in all you can embrace. Everything lies within My realm of thinking."

The novice went on to say, "Speak out against agnostic and atheistic thinking; inculcate into man's mind that evil breeds contempt and more evil and that happiness lies within mankind's mind if only he can just accept happiness. Even though the laws and rules created by men on this Earth may often try your patience—as they want to rule you—man still can continue to think happy thoughts each day of his life knowing the Father is ever with him and in the end it will be *"Thy will be done, O God, Thy will."*

LIFE ON EARTH IS A SCHOOL
THE FATHER'S GIFTS TO MANKIND

Have you not wondered how mankind learned to speak aloud? Have you not wondered how mankind began to think? Have you not speculated about the health of the temple, one's body? Who is responsible for all this? The answer, of course, is God.

We are going to bring to you today some thoughts man should ponder over long and hard!

Has man thought that his present life on Earth is meant as a school for learning? "Learning what?" you ask. If you read carefully all the lessons we have brought to you the journey of discovery will take you from the time before your birth—to living on Earth—then to life after death. The lessons will help you live with all the confusion found in between these concepts.

When the Lord sent the first bird onto Earth, He requested that we listen to the song of the bird, that soon we would be able to lift our heads and have beautiful sounds of music issuing forth.   He taught us not to despair--that He would be in constant attendance to us until we learned to decipher the mental thoughts which He had placed into our minds.   He also promised us a temple, a body which He created for individuals, and He promised that as long as we cared for our body with the foods He would supply for us, they would be healthy.

Since the beginning of time, the Lord has tried to re-acquaint us with the *Original Lessons* He had taught us.   He promised us that remnants of the original *Truths* would forever remain alive within our minds, and He has kept His promise-- even though we do not consciously recognize all of the *Laws* or all of the lessons.   We instinctively live many of those *Truths* learned during many of our lives.   The Father continues to bring only love and good into our lives, and He will follow us throughout all eternity.   The Lord lives closer to us than we can ever imagine, for He is within our minds, He is within our hearts, and within our every breath that we take.

One of the lessons He originally taught us was never to despair, that He was within easy reach of our thoughts and our hearts, and that--even though negativity would try to substitute thoughts into our minds--the Lord assured us that we were not to despair:

> *"Abide within Me, live with Me. Rejoice, for I am within your aching heart, within the widow's weeds and I shall continue to sit alongside thee until the end of time everlasting. Just come unto Me."*

My child, salute the Lord each morning by acknowledging His presence, then knowing full well in your heart that He is there living closely with us and He is able to aid and abide within us. The closer we live with Him and the more we love Him, the more love He sends to us.

Dear child, let me serve as an example for that which you should always strive to be. Take this time, as I do, for this beautiful lesson the Father has sent unto you as you live on the Earth. Just as the Lord says:

> *"I shall accompany you forever and ever for in your heartaches, I, too, feel your pain; but Truth shall always prevail and from My Truth springs other Truths until, eventually, all of My children shall have the complete Truths instilled into all of their hearts. They shall know that Truth must advance Truth, and this land upon which you live will have the most advanced Truths and instructions that have ever been known. So, let man be*

content with that promise and allow My love to live within you forever.   *Amen."*

THE LORD FEELS OUR HEARTACHE

The Father will never let us walk alone if He feels our heartaches. He will find ways to alleviate them. We must have faith in the Father, and not only learn His *Truths*, but we must live and teach them.

Love is the answer to all life. We must learn to love our "self" first. If we feel love for ourselves, we then can feel His love and the love our fellowman extends to us; in this way, we can live with love in our hearts and souls. The Father uses our light wisely and asks that we continue to do likewise with His. If we are bothered by certain problems, we must learn to ask the Lord for the answers or the directions that we might take to alleviate the problem or heartache.

Many men come back to live on the Earth actually hating the Lord God Almighty because they were not able to resolve their own problems or thinking in another lifetime. They feel remiss in their thinking ill of the Father but, nonetheless, they continue to hate Him in vain. Love is all that the Father understands. If man is ever to evolve to a higher state of being, he must let go of the hatred. Man must learn to face himself each morning, with joy in his heart. He then can ask for directions, guidance and explanations as to why he feels as he does and why things have gone wrong in his daily life.

There are ministers who teach so-called *Truths* and who cling to their single solitary philosophy even if evil prevails because of them. They continue to teach man the same kind of hatred and evil. Those same ministers who demonstrate against the *Everlasting Truths* will eventually be forgiven by the Father, even though they have placed a cloud over His *Truths*. He is most forgiving for He is the personification of love.

Some of the cults that exist today started out on the right road, but then they became involved with material things and power; they started teaching half-truths so that they might control man's mind. The leaders of these cults sought refuge from the Lord as well. They never came asking the Lord for His advice. They instead always called out to their own Angels to help them, for they wanted the Angels to agree with what they were promoting. Thus the adverse conditions that exist today are the result of having distorted the *Truth* to mean what they wanted it to mean, not as the Lord has taught. When these ministers or teachers are exposed for their materialistic ways or exposed as impostors, many live in shame and anger thereafter. These ministers show hatred toward the Father by cursing and accusing the Father for causing them to stumble and fall.

It is only when the fallen attempt to rise again and face the truth within themselves that they recover immediately from hatred of the Father and they at once begin to seek and understand *"Truth."* If they are honest men, they explore other avenues of teaching and will ask forgiveness of those they have wronged. It is the deceitful minister who hates to admit his wrongs or that he was capable of teaching untruths and will not admit that he cannot reconcile his teachings and thinking with the Lord. He will have to repeat his life over and over again until he can reconcile his teachings with the *Everlasting Truth.* He has a hard row to hoe for these ministers of the so-called *Truth* can inflame a whole community, into doing vice and evil. Thus they too respond to that force of evil rather than the higher source of energy. The Masters say, "Give unto others *Truth* always, teach them only *Truth* and avoid the holocausts that come into lives of men who teach evil."

YOU WERE ALLOWED TO LIVE AGAIN

Whenever a person feels close to the Lord, the Lord feels close to him. The Father asks for our forgiveness for assuming we could remember all of His *Laws*; that is why He continually tries to teach them to us during each lifetime. The Father stands very close to us and through examining our minds, He begins to understand how difficult it has been for many men to live through the holocausts. Many men have had to endure holocausts over and over again. As in His *Original Laws*, He begged us to extend our hands to the next person and teach him all the *Truths* we know. That is the responsibility we accepted and promised to do many centuries ago. The Father begins to understand the deviations among men. He observes the various and sundry types of men who now occupy the Earth and sees the differences in the levels of their evolution. It is no wonder that some of us live apart from one another, but we must learn to accept life and man's differences as it is and not consider it a defeat. Help man to see that joy and happiness can survive within his mind no matter what happens to him.

Evolution is a subject man refuses to talk about or try to understand for it is easier for him to accept the deviations among men as circumstantial. We must bear in mind that it is difficult for man to remember who or what they were in another lifetime; thus, man evolves slowly in accepting the precedence that he once knew well. There were precedences that he understood and others did not. Many who instilled these *Truths* into their own minds are determined to keep that information to themselves alone. Evidence of this flames forth, evidence of *Truth Everlasting* has dying embers because man refuses to allow his mind to accept the idea of *Life* and *Truth Everlasting*. Many men refuse to live close to the Father. Man does not understand that with the Father's help, he can relearn and reinforce his own thinking, which will allow his mind to function on the highest level. He refuses to bend in this thinking and refuses to send his mind forth to relearn and to seek the *Truths*. Man thus constrains his mind and stifles the amount of energy and learning that could come to him.

He who salutes the Lord each morning wishing for joy and

happiness finds it. Believe me, my child, when I declare that He will reward those living close to Him and those who request the *Original Laws* will have them instilled into their minds.

According to these precepts, man was allowed to live once more so the original thoughts could be inculcated into his mind. The Father says:

> *"If We deliver you from evil, why then do you not try to deliver yourself from evil by abiding within the precepts offered to you? Why do you not live like the Law says: Come unto Me and sacrifice your life no more?"*

Those were the original words spoken by the Father, but men refused to understand their meaning. What He was trying to say is, *"Come unto Me; use the Laws; use your life wisely; and come back safely to Me."*

These are known as non-violent times; but in accordance with our viewpoint here, more violence is occurring at any one moment than ever before in recorded history. While it is true that you must account only for your own actions, man must also try to stop others from hurting one another. Man must learn to accept the Father into his life and live close to Him everyday. If he does that, it will afford him a peaceful solution to all things.

We do not understand why man does not take advantage of this and live according to the *Laws*.

Men were set free, all equal, no servants, no live-in maids and no slaves. Who started the system of bartering off men and women? We all suffer the consequence of bartering off one soul to another soul. In the same vein, who started nations fighting among each other? Until we can honestly answer these questions, we have little chance of understanding the history of mankind.

HE MET A SENILE OLD MAN
(A Parable)

One of the men who had been taught all the *Original Laws* continued to repeat them to himself many times during the day so that he would remember them all. Since he was a wandering man, he met many different individuals and he would constantly ask these men if they would teach him any new *Truths* that they had learned. Then one day during one of his solitary trips, he came upon an old man whom he classified as being senile because this old man said little and seemed unimpressed by the wanderer's conversation. As it later turned out, he was more sane than the wanderer.

The wanderer asked his same request of the old man as he had of all he met during his wanderings: "Please teach me any new *Truths* that you might have learned during your years on Earth, old man. Please repeat to me all you have learned so that I might realize different thoughts from those that I remember." The old man looked at him curiously and then responded, "You, who are new in my life, you have come to me. Now you repeat to me all the *Original Truths* as you have remembered them." The wandering man did as he was bid and elucidated upon each and every *Truth*. He repeated them correctly, even with the very intonations that he had remembered.

The supposedly senile old man then asked, "Why do you want to learn more *Truths* than you already know? Have you not already repeated them all correctly to me?"

The wanderer, who was considered a wise man, answered by saying, "Wise men need to know more and more; otherwise their wisdom will wilt and wane if one does not continue using his mind."

"Continue then," the old one replied, "to say the *Original*

Truths each morning and night and teach them to others. I further commission you this day to oversee the *Original Teachings* and do not omit one word as you repeat them to others."

The wanderer set out again down the pathway that somehow led him directly into the company of the senile old man again. "Do not stumble or fall, my son," said the old man as he departed; "Understand, my son, how hard it is to hear and to learn all the *Truths* you remember so well."

The wanderer continued down his same pathway that he thought would lead him safely back home because he was preparing to find his way home to the Father. He repeated the *Truths* daily, morning and night, and continued to teach all he met.

Then one day, he stumbled over his own feet and remembered the old man's warning. He began to look up into the sky as if talking with the Father. He said, "That senile old man helped me renew my faith in You, Father, but he was an old, senile man; how could he know whether I spoke the *Truth* or whether I have strayed from the *Truth*?" Then a bolt of lightning hit his pathway and again he stumbled and fell. When he looked up, he saw the face of the Father above him and then he understood that the Father had caused him to stumble and fall so that he could indeed see His face again for this was his reward for spreading the *Truths* to others.

The Father asked why the wanderer had felt the senile old man could not have known the *Truths*. "My objection to what happened is that you judged your fellowman—you called him senile. All the time it was I walking in his shoes; I was that senile old man. I wanted to test you to determine how you feel about your fellowman. It is true you have learned My *Laws* and *Lessons* so well, but you have much to learn about living with them. The felony was compounded because you teach My *Laws* without thoroughly understanding them. Learn, My son; do not look for other new *Laws* to learn. Learn to correctly use the original ones I have taught you."

THE KING AND THE PEON

(A Parable)

An *Angel of Truth* descended to Earth dressed like a slave and approached a renowned king. He advised the king about the lessons on *Truth Everlasting* which he could and was willing to teach the king. The king looked down upon the peon and said, "How do you know more about *Truth Everlasting* than I do, for am I not a king?"

Soon another *Angel of Truth* came to the Earth to see the king; this Angel was dressed as a missionary, but he too was rejected. The king shouted, "How dare they think they can teach me more than I already know, for am I not a king? Indeed, because I am the king, the Lord must have taught me everything I should ever need to know!"

Then suddenly one day the king died. When he entered into the *Kingdom of Heaven (or "The Land of Light")* he realized his mistake for there he saw the Lord surrounded by the so-called peon and missionary. It was then that he realized that the Lord had indeed sent these messengers to him to help enlighten him.

The lesson the king was meant to learn was to allow

changes in his thinking to come about through the teachings of the Lord and His Teachers. One never knows in what form they will appear. Each man must teach that evil does not pay, as sooner or later they too will walk the same pathway as did the king. In this instance, he learned too late that the *Truth* is ever evident around man. If man turns a deaf ear to *Truth*, he will regret it in the later lifetimes. He will have to live with it on the Earth as well as in *"The Land of Light."*

We must not turn away from any man. He may be a messenger from God. Thus, we should treat all people equally with dignity. We must evaluate the messenger's words. We all know right from wrong. If it doesn't ring true then question your higher self.

THE DIRT FARMER
(A Parable)

We wish you would always remember this story about the dirt farmer who was selected by the Lord to be His messenger among men. As the Lord presented Himself to the farmer each morning a new Truth was taught and continued to be taught until the farmer understood it completely. The Lord had told the farmer that when he had learned all the *Truths,* the Father would no longer present Himself to him.

Then one morning when the Father did not present Himself to the farmer, he knew that it was time for him to set out upon the trail to teach man all the lessons that the Lord had brought to him. Even though the wheat that he had planted was nearing the time for harvest, he knew he had to be about his Father's business and that the wheat would have to wait.

The farmer set sail to teach men along the way the *Truth* as he had been taught; but in essence each time he spoke among men, he was embroiled in controversy, and they refused to listen to him. "What do you know," they chided, "you are only a dirt farmer? How dare you expose us to what you call *Truth?* You are not of our equal! You are just a dirt farmer!"

Being reminded of this every day, he felt defamed and dishonored by these men until finally he began to feel ashamed of being a dirt farmer. Suddenly one day, he thought: "I do not need to be abused any more." He returned his farm to harvest his own wheat. He had tried but failed to teach the essence of *Truth* to his fellowmen. He felt that he had failed the

Lord.

The Lord was not dismayed by his failure. He called the farmer back to the top of the mountain, and there He continued to re-teach him in a simpler manner so that everyone would understand what he was saying. He instructed the farmer to return home and practice this new way of teaching upon his own family. As soon as each member of his family understood his teachings, he was to set out again to do the Father's work. The Father said unto him:

> "Be not dismayed, My son, by their thinking and conversation nor the treatment that you receive. Say to them, 'The Lord took me on high and motivated me again in a different manner. The Lord feels closer to each man who believes in His Truths Everlasting."

Obediently, the farmer set sail again to teach still another group of men. This time the farmer understood more about the men he spoke to than they did themselves. He pointed out their weaknesses as well as shared his own; he showed them their better sides and how they could cultivate them even more. He taught them to salute the Lord each morning and in so doing, on several occasions, he felt the presence of the Father around him.

As he spoke to one group after another, the August Figure of the Lord was dismayed that these men would not allow themselves to release their own negative thoughts and would not allow themselves to learn the *Truths* that He had sent forth with the farmer. His dismay finally led to disgust. He became so offended by man that, in a relatively short time, He withdrew from those men completely. He withdrew His presence but watched over them from afar hoping they would learn and appreciate His Teachings. When their crops failed for lack of rain, His heart hurt for them, but they would not seek help from Him. He truly hoped that at some future occasion they would simply find their way back home alone.

Thus, my children, those men have to find their way back home alone because they rejected His *Original Teachings* for had He not sent His farmer messenger to teach them?

HOW TO HEAL THYSELF

We would like this lesson to be given to all mankind who at one time or another suffered some type of physical or emotional illness.

Do not stack the deck of cards against yourself. Instead think positively, "I will accept my condition for I know I shall be healed. My lifetime on Earth shall not be lived as one of despair. All will be well. I shall tell my body to let go of negativity, and come back to its normal state of being."

Affairs and conditions set up man's mind to accept the spiritual side of things. So do not despair; say nothing negative to the Father. Say only:

> "I feel badly about what has happened to me, but I accept it and want to go on living within my haven of refuge until finally all cells interact, not in a negative way, but only in a good and positive health-giving manner. Please, O Heavenly Father, direct my energy within my cells to respond to this way of thinking so that I might accept life and know in truth Thy meaning of 'heal thyself.'   Amen"

ACCEPTANCE

In the beginning we were shown pictures to teach us how to learn through sight; then sound was added so that we were able to use two of God's gifts. Man can only chew so much food in his mouth at one time. If he bites off too big a chunk of food, he must spit it out or choke and lose his life. So it is with life. This analogy applies to learning, also. Man must educate his mind to accepting that which can be changed in his life and disposing of what cannot be changed. He has to learn to live with what he cannot change, but he can make it a lot easier if he asks God to help him after he has gone with the problem as far as he can go.

Man must live his life to the best of his ability, facing every challenge that presents itself each moment of his existence; disposing of those things that he cannot change allows him to work harder on the more positive parts of his life. Each man must instill into his own mind the depth of his perception—how deep is down--and the height of his own consciousness—how high is up? When this is not done, he can and will fall to whatever depths of depression that he allows himself to fall. Desperate men who have not taken their consciousness to greater heights allow only trouble to enter their consciousness, while the active thinking man has learned to challenge his own existence by looking only to God and his always-present inner happiness.

This morning, we showed you a river flowing comfortably, easily, peacefully and harmoniously between two high mountains. Man must learn to allow his life to flow as easily with his acceptance of all facets of life. He must learn to calm his heart, calm his soul, and flow with the tide of time, similar to the river as it allows the high and low tides to carry it through rocks and shoals. Do not increase your heartaches. Just listen to the river flowing beneath your feet or imagine yourself standing atop the highest mountain. It seems the heartaches and worries disappear. Man determines his own speed at which he is allowed to function. Man responds to the urging by his Master Teachers. So it is with all of mankind. We must urge him on to find his "haven of refuge." We must vigilantly avoid the holocausts that come into our personal lives as well as into our lands.

Learn to lead a happy, normal life from now until the end of your lifetime. Simply said, it is to enjoy each moment each day and rejoice at the gift of your good health and happiness. Feel the Divine Presence within your mind, heart and soul. And often declare, *"Amen."*

WHEN WE LIVED AS TRIBESMEN

His August figure loomed ahead of us in the beginning of time; and when we sensed His presence, we became wildly excited and alert. We blessed His loving countenance for we so wanted to be able to realign our thinking with His so that He could communicate with us. It was possible at that time to align His mind with our thoughts and we were then able to listen to Him. As time went on, a change took place—a revolution of sorts began in our minds—we suddenly discovered, due to our having discarded the Father's *Truths* that we were unable to communicate with Him. There was a shared sense of loss that prevailed within our minds. We became fearful for we felt lost without our ability to communicate with Him, our Father.

We were a proud people. We sat down and tried to reconstruct our thinking processes. We thought we could reconstruct our thoughts from the very beginning of time, but the Father's messages became fainter and fainter with time, and so re-education seemed the only possible way to retrieve His *Laws*.

We would then seek out the wiser men of the tribe and ask that the Father's lessons be repeated; but, ignorant as we were, we did not understand their mumbling. We erroneously thought they were actually teaching us the true lessons again. Despairing that we had been deliberately misled by the Leaders and Teachers, we resigned to living alone. They had wanted to control our thinking; thus, they taught us incorrectly. When their ploys were discovered by the Father, the Teachers were punished and the *Original Lessons* were removed from their minds. Since there was not one lesson left within their minds, they were neither able to teach us correctly nor to use them for themselves. When they discovered the error of their ways, they tried to single out one *Truth* that they would be able to remember. They thought they could refine one thought so the Father would no longer hide His face from them. In response, the Father announced again these words to them: *"If you do not teach each man correctly, you will no longer be a teacher. And never again will you see My face before you during your years on Earth."*

They, in turn, announced to mankind, "We have seen the Father again and He has disciplined us and has instructed us to remember all the *Truths* that He taught us, and He has told us to assemble all of mankind and teach them in a correct fashion with no deception whatsoever." Thus, we understood once again that the Father loved us all, and He was concerned for us, but once He discovered that which was being taught to us was not the *Truth,* He withdrew from us completely but watched from afar. He then sent word to us by a messenger of *Truth* that He would no longer live close beside us and could not help us again to the extent that He had done in the past. It was up to us to relearn the lessons correctly.

This messenger of *Truth* assured us the Father was seeking a release from us and although He wanted us to see His face, He could not allow His teachings to be taught in an erroneous manner as they are being taught today. If mankind desires to see the Father's face again, he must make the effort to learn the *Truths* and bless the Lord each morning with warmth and delight, trying to live closer to Him than ever before.

Within man's heart he knows this is true—that the Lord loves each of us individually, but most of all, He loves those of us who pass along the Father's wisdom seeking to help their fellow man. If man saves one man, he saves a hundred in the eyes of the Lord.

OVERCOMING FEAR

If we could overcome but one evil, we would be assured of happiness. That evil is fear—fear of tomorrow, fear of the atom bomb, fear of old age and fear of loneliness. Overcome fear and we all could be serene and happy living with peace and harmony. Instead, we find one man pitted against another only because of fear. It is possible to overcome fear through concentration on God and forsaking all things leading to self-gratification.

We were not meant to live like animals merely existing within the pack of society. Rather, each man was created as a complete unit exemplifying the perfection of God's love. We fear other men simply because we do not understand them as they evolve under their own pattern. In God's eyes, all patterns are recognizable because it is He who is the designer. We, in our limited way, will sit in judgment of another because of fear. He differs from us, perhaps in color, creed or race. Thus we choose to fear him, dislike him and distrust him. Learn to look with God's eyes, speak with God's lips and hear with God's ears. When this is sincerely practiced, there will be no man who cannot say, "I have not found a man I cannot like." Under *God's Laws,* all men are whole and all are perfect. By perceiving it so, it is automatically made complete.

We need more love, genuine love—not self-seeking love—to beam upon the world. We are not lost in this century even after having lived with fears. We must ask for forgiveness for allowing ourselves to entertain fear and God will forgive and send more love. If fears were scrutinized closely, we would find them to be only wisps of smoke that soon vanish into the air.

Fear is not part of us. It is nothing that God has sent. It is insidious only because it seems real. Fear is only a mirage, however, and there is nothing to fear but fear itself.

God created us to surrender the whole living of our lives to Him and to live in peace and happiness with complete faith in His goodness and management of our affairs.

MANY MINISTERS LIVING TODAY

The Father tries to help man find answers to his prayers, and the thoughts that roam within his mind. Man, whether he is conscious of it or not is constantly seeking after the *Truth.* The avenue of *Truth* is lined with trees of thoughts and thought waves. Think about it this way: If you do not stop along the street to view the trees, how can you see the answers to those thoughts found hanging from the upper tree limbs? What is meant here is that you must stop and ponder about a thought then sort out the different possibilities proffered to you and send them out into the ether. Man must then be patient and wait for the answers to be sent and finally allow his mind the freedom of selecting the correct answer.

Today, allow us to speak with you about current religion. As we see it from our point of view, falsehoods are taught today straight from the Bible. The interpreted face value of these teachings is false. God never sent such edicts as we see taught in Bible classes today. How can peace be upheld in an orderly fashion when the so-called original promises are so misinterpreted? First one minister and then another interprets God's words in different ways, and it is their interpretations which account for hurt and disillusionment of their flocks and sometimes cause them to cease being participants in any formal religion. Some members become so confused that they leave the congregations for fear of losing their minds. This type of false education alone does not then set them free from what they have originally been taught. Those positive flowers are on the periphery while the desert flowers bloom deep within their souls and they are planted there permanently. So, who wins and who loses? The God above resents this sort of thinking and teachings. He accuses mankind of ill-advice, false teachings and maltreatment of their flocks. He notices that ministers are seeking permission to direct their congregates' lives by dominating their thinking. The Father accuses them also of evil intent, of using their minds in a negative fashion only to control the minds of their congregants and He feels that materialism is often too great a part of each service.

The Lord searches among the so-called righteous men and women, striving to find an honest person among them. In His search for an honest man, He will first eliminate any minister who is supposed to be serving mankind but instead educates people to see the devil within themselves; this invites the congregation to feel the devil in their midst. This is often done in sermons by expanding upon all sorts of punishments for mankind should they not obey the minister completely. By the constant brainwashing of "hell and damnation," man often begins to accuse himself of all sorts of evil acts. He inculcates these thoughts deep into his mind over and over again until he can find no peace of mind even when trying to rest. Man becomes absolutely sure that his soul will eventually belong to the devil or some evil source. We who live in the light know that there is no hell or devil, only positive and negative thoughts.

How can the *Truths* be inculcated into these poor congregants' minds to wipe out the evil thoughts? We are constantly reminded not to "accuse man of evil intent" for these seeds were planted directly into his mind by the so-called ministers of *Truth* who constantly seek holocausts upon the Earth through their teachings. Their educating and teachings are false, and God alone will remind them of this when they return to Him after passing through the veil.

God loves us all and is despondent to see how His children are driven from pillar to post seeking a glimmer of light because the religious education they receive is limited to the devil or hell and threats such as predictions: "If you do not do thus-and-so, you will land in hell." There is no such place as hell. One struggles hard enough on the Earth to learn his lessons so that he may occasionally refer to it as "living in hell," but he creates it for himself. Man should turn back the pages of history and reread the ancient teachings; perhaps the answers to *Truth* and life would then abound within his mind so that he would find peaceful co-existence on Earth with all of mankind.

THE MOLTEN LAVA

My child, we are going to bring to you a picture, and this picture will demonstrate God's love and the way into the universe. Look very closely at the molten lava because we do not want you to forget the lesson of the lava. A man who has viewed a lava flow from a volcano will never forget the redness of the color of the lava and how it very quickly finds a pathway down the mountain, forming new soil.

The Father teaches us to live close to the edge of the molten lava called Earth. He taught us not to tread upon the lava and not to try to climb the mountain to get to the top immediately. The important feature of the lesson is that man could always say, "Father, I am afraid of the lava. Please help me avoid being taken into the flow." Man doesn't understand he has nothing to fear because when the lava was flowing, the Father stood by assigning direction to the flow. He never would have allowed the holocausts that could have happened. So man's prayers should be:

"Show me the way, Father. I must learn to trust in Your instructions and in Your instincts completely. Thus, I shall never know fear as I know You are ever present to help me avoid the pitfalls and holocausts that come into man's life. Amen"

What we want you to remember is that man finds time and gives time to what he loves. How can he say that he loves the Father if he has not learned to greet him each morning, to trust His decisions, and to follow His guidance each day? If children need unconditional love--which the Father always truly extends to us—why then can we not extend unconditional love to Him?

If as we have been taught that parents are models and if man does not love himself, how then can man expect his children to love themselves or to love God? If man does not love himself, how can he truly love God? Why can man not understand that God is within him? That flick of light that differentiates each man personifies God and synonymous with God is the word _love_. If man does not love himself, then he and only he creates the dysfunctional families. God despairs when He sees that mankind does not attempt to live His _Laws_ even fifteen percent of the time! The Father says it is all right to make mistakes. It is through mistakes that we learn. But many of man's mistakes would not have to occur if he would open his heart and mind to the Father and ask for His guidance and direction on a daily basis.

The man who cannot admit his mistakes or admit that it is even possible for him to make mistakes is the man who is saying, "Look at me. Am I not God?" How many have you known in this lifetime who will never admit they have made a mistake? The lesson we wish mankind would learn is that the moment he refuses to admit he has made a mistake, he will kill what the Father has blessed him with—the creativity of learning. Then the man stumbles on and on, generation after generation, until he finally learns to be humble, that it is possible to admit mistakes because it is a healthy emotion. God will forgive man any mistakes he makes if man will only admit the mistake and then forgive himself for making it.

Can you imagine the heat of the molten lava? Can you imagine how it can sear not just the skin but the soul of mankind? His soul endures a hurt as deep as the lava burns when he refuses to accept the Father as his partner and guiding light. The soul of man seeks help but man's conscious mind refuses to liberate the soul from its pain.

It is by trial and error that man learns *Truth*. It is not an exact science that can be taught, as men like to think. As we mentioned before, it is only learned through trial and error. "How deep is down? How high is up?" These are not scientific questions alone. The Father means for us to learn the meanings of this through trial and error, so the lessons will both be learned and endured. No, it is not a password of any kind. There is an actual *Truth* governing this mental possibility, for that truthfully is what it is.

When man learns a new thought or idea, he should use it wisely—meaning that he should not keep the thought for himself alone, but instead should share it with those people who he knows could be interested in the discussion of the new thought or idea. Each man's responsibility is to teach other men how to use the light, meaning the *Truth*, and how to understand its true meaning. It is <u>each man's responsibility</u> to reach out and help his fellow man not only in a material way but also in a spiritual way. We know that this will make little sense to you until you begin to think on a broader scope. "How deep is down," is an actual equation of how to use our mind's eye correctly. This will give you something to think about.

THE TAPESTRY OF LIFE

Who among you really knows the true meaning of "the tapestry of life"? What does it actually mean to you when you hear the words spoken? We have to first understand that in the very beginning of time, we agreed to accomplish certain things. First, we conferred with our council and the hierarchy, who on a daily basis were trying to help us direct our lives along the lines that we had promised to accomplish. They did not interfere in our selection of duties. We assumed all of the responsibility ourselves. We were egotistical enough to believe that when we returned to Earth, promising to finish all we had left undone, that we could handle all our problems and accomplish all our promises without the Father's help.

We had forgotten the expression often heard, "Time is of the essence in life." We forgot that the past *is* the future and the future is the past; and that if we do not learn from the past, we are doomed to repeat it again and again.

All men descend upon the Earth to finish old business and to reweave his *Tapestry of Life*, but he arrives upon his own plane of thought similar to the one he used before.

Man Finds Himself in Trouble When Alone

We soon found ourselves in deep trouble for we had not understood the depth of the responsibilities that we had assigned and assumed for ourselves. When we realized we were in trouble, we were fraught with anxiety, which only added to our discomfiture, and it appeared as a real calamity which prevented us from enjoying little of our lifetime on Earth.

Because of all this discomfiture, we began to reward ourselves by denying that we had any problems. We set about convincing ourselves that we were indeed wise men and that we did not need anyone else's help, that soon we would find a way out of this maze, and a new direction would come so that we could live happily again. We felt that by denial we would be able to heal our own wounds. Upon realization that we were in trouble, we began to demonstrate to the Father that our need of His light and His guidance was even greater than we had once thought.

The Father reminded us that man had accepted his own original pattern of life before rebirth. There was a certain predetermined pattern he was to follow and that must be completed before death. If he doesn't assume control of his life so as to finish his pattern, he will die owing a great debt. Man's transportation back home is assured, but his luggage of unfulfilled thoughts and unrealized deeds are unacceptable for the voyage back.

One's Tapestry of Life May Need Reweaving

Alas! We had completely forgotten about the accumulation of our errors from past lifetimes that had left certain parts of the tapestry unwoven or in disrepair. Thus in each lifetime, we are simply trying to avoid creating any new errors while concentrating our attention on healing old wounds and settling old scores in such a positive nature that we would not have any more unwoven parts added to our tapestry of life hanging over our heads.

This is how men became so involved in the problems they are living today. When man became so complacent and so full of ego, he envisioned his lifetime on Earth as being whole and complete, yet he finds unravelings from some previous lifetimes occurring again and again. We learn from this disrepair from past lifetimes that we must remedy the ideas and thoughts that we place into our minds. It is our minds that can defeat us as much as the erroneous deeds we perform. Occasionally, we find a reward for ourselves by thinking the pleasant and positive thoughts rather than the negative and hateful ones relating to our fellowmen.

We must curb our appetite for food as well as for gossip, for the fat inhibits our thinking positively and from also liking ourselves. We must continue to talk and think over traumas that come in everyday living and thereby evaluate our lifetime on this Earth. In so doing, we are trying to remedy our thinking of other people. It is hopeless to continue being negative and holding grudges against one another—it simply destroys our light. We do not know the pathway our fellowman chose.

Allow Man to Live as He Chooses

Allow man his freedom of thought; allow man freedom to live as he chooses for if we do not learn this lesson, happenstance brings it back into our lives again and again. So extend a peaceful happy smile to all of mankind and be certain to extend this love from your very heart and soul and make it as sincere as the smile. You must love every man. You do not have to like him or his way of life, but you must respect his freedom of choice.

Life would be a far happier adventure to live if each man perceived his brother's heartache. There is not a man who lives who does not have pressures. How wonderful it would be if we would reach out to our fellowman and offer sustenance and understanding of his heartache.

Love the Lord with All Your Heart

My children, ask yourself, "How can I become a better person if I am to survive on this Earth? How can I become a better person within my heart and soul?" Examine yourself each day, but do not allow yourself to be despondent if you find vacancies, in your thinking or actions or feel you are not weaving your tapestry correctly. Over here there are many rules to follow when examining your heart and soul; but by committing to memory this one thought, life can become a lot easier:

> *"Live close to your Father; ask His forgiveness in all that you commit against mankind. Ask for help in reversing any negativity you might feel about man and life. Hold the Father in high esteem and love Him with all of your heart and soul. Let your mind worship Him freely whenever the opportunity presents itself."*

Commit this to memory and continue striving to fulfill your destiny, alone if necessary, but you must finish that which you began centuries ago knowing that *Truth* prevails on Earth as well as in heaven.

Remember, when we accept defeat, we allow our brain to operate on the lower level and we allow ourselves to become depressed. In so doing, we allow our immune system to depress itself and we set ourselves up for all kinds of allergies and illnesses.

Man Is His Own Obstacle to Success

The Lord has compassion for all human beings and yearns for their success. Thus, He allows them to live many times. To be able to accept this philosophy, we must understand fully His thinking, His way of fulfilling your prayers and His aspirations for all of us. He loves us more than any human is capable of loving one another, and thus He strives to help us find that success to fulfill our lives. It is always within our reach. We have the instincts to find that haven of refuge in our minds that can lead to our success. The obstacles that stand in man's way, keeping him from attaining success, are within his own mind for he is never hindered by the Father. Man is his own hindrance— his own worst enemy. We must hold steadfastly to the realization that man can change. Each day is a new beginning and with that comes HOPE and the reweaving of our *Tapestry of Life*.

SUCCESSFUL LIVING

Successful living can be attained through faith in something bigger than materialism and men. It must be faith in God. Give a man all his heart's desires and leave out his soul's growth and I give you a man living in a wasteland. We seek and search all our lives through for a better unity with our higher self. That is called communication with our God. A man who is living faith is a man with a purpose.

We are always conscious of the disunited people who are aimlessly wandering through a maze of self-deception and confusion. First, they run after self-gratification—the I, Me, and Mine Syndrome. Then the senses turn feverishly to materialism, always finding ashes of discontent, never knowing why they feel as if they are the "Legion of the Damned." This is not new. We had this condition with us even before the stories of the nations were recorded. We want to believe this is a harder and more complex century in which we live. Nothing is farther from the *Truth;* we are living nothing new. All this has happened before—wars, selfishness, and political machinations. All this existed before and they were dangers faced by all people. These problems must be faced and overcome by every generation. Out of darkness and the great suffering of nations comes rebirth. As a civilization is likened to a giant boat that gathers barnacles--every so often the hull must be scraped or the boat would be swamped by the accumulating parasites.

So it is, my children, with our souls. We take on the parasitical evils and then we must rid ourselves of them so that we might survive. It has ever been so and it will continue always to be this cycle. Do not live in fear of the present-day evils. Take unto yourself faith that will bring you through with a courage and a serenity that nothing can shake. These days must be lived through and they will be, with both our faith and our partnership with God. Through Him we all can come out better and wiser people who can create a definite beginning for a better world.

LOVE BEGETS LOVE

Each morning the Father touches our minds and tries to teach us about the *Original Truths*. But more than that, if we will listen quietly, He will also try to guide and direct us for that day. Thus, He has instructed us to live one moment at a time, one hour and one day at a time. If we have faith and believe in the Father, He will guide us through everything we have to face before it happens.

In the morning after He communes with us, He sets us free again to start a new beginning. He teaches us to forgive ourselves for whatever has previously occurred. In forgiving ourselves, we truly are beginning anew. He orders us to forgive and forget, but we can only accomplish this if we believe in and understand His lessons.

Man somehow has forgotten that when the Father touches in with him each morning, He is sending back the energy that sets each of us free to function at our own level each day. Without His energy we cannot exist nor complete the purpose of our lives. The Father hopes that, by extending our energy level, we can also extend our imaginations a little farther into the universe so as to extend our minds and our consciousness. We can only hope to fulfill our purpose and fulfill the covenant we promised Him before rebirth by expanding our consciousness to the highest level of intelligence. Since our lives down on the Earth are compared to a school, we must truly learn the lessons offered from each occurrence in our lives and use it to further our climb up the steps of life.

Mistakes Teach Us

If man understands that there is a lesson that he must learn from every mistake he makes, he will sift through every step he took before the mistake occurred. Once he sees and understands his own frailties, he will not have to repeat that part of his life or that error again. Then he must put it out of his mind completely, using that period of time after he explored the steps that caused his downfall as a catharsis to cleanse his mind so that he can put that experience behind him and wholly forget it. We are taught that we must cleanse our minds so that we can profit from the new experiences that come to us each day of our lives.

In relationship with other people, we must always remember that we must learn to also forgive and forget. We must remember that love begets love while hatred begets hatred. Also, we must remember that in our relationship with the Father, He will reward us with whatever we extend to Him. The Lord loves all His children and, therefore, gives freely to those who extend love to Him in great abundance.

This is a *Universal Law*, indeed one of the ancient *Laws*, and should, therefore, be observed by all mankind. Man should remember that by hating someone else, it will return tenfold to him. Knowing this, does it not make sense to wipe our consciousness clear of all hatred and send forth love so that it, too, can be returned tenfold?

If man truly wants to feel loved, he has been taught that before he arises from bed each morning, to lie in bed, calmly, saying nothing and listening. As soon as he sends love and rejoicing for the experience of another day, he will suddenly feel great warmth for the Lord within him will fill the man's heart and soul with His love. As he is enjoying this experience, the faith that he feels shows the Father his loyalty which is what the Father is seeking from all His children. Man, in turn, will be rewarded with the love and compassion that he has been needing while living on the Earth.

The Father not only promises His children a heavenly abode in which they may dwell when they return to His conscious state, He has also promised us a heavenly abode here on Earth if we but have faith in Him and live His Laws.

When you return through the veil, you will find that heavenly abode in which you will be allowed to live with Him, as well as the Honor Hall of Justice. The love there amounts to more love and divine presence than man is capable of feeling. We say to you and to all mankind, avoid feelings of loneliness. Truly feel loved and know in truth that, with the Lord, all is love and genuine kindliness. He wishes us happiness and joy. All that He asks for in return is that we believe in Him and send Him daily our love and caring. In turn, He rewards us fully by helping us find a haven of refuge within our minds and helps us to seek a peaceful coexistence on Earth as is found in His heavenly grace.

AFFIRMATIONS

Celebrate life, my child; celebrate life and living. Few men understand the true meaning of the words "celebrate" or "celebration." Each morning upon awakening, say unto the Lord:

"I celebrate life, Father. I thank You for my health, my happiness and my joy. I celebrate life because You have helped me expand my consciousness so that I have no fear of living while on the Earth. Help me by guiding my footsteps so that I do not stumble and fall. Show me the way that brings rewards into my life for my manifestations of the Truth that equality is for all of mankind."

Celebrate life! Find it inviting, exhilarating and joyous! Celebrate life!

Now if each man upon awakening each morning would begin his day by saying:

"I feel blessed by Thee, Lord. I feel blessed by Thee. I am willing to abdicate control over my entire life. Thus,

all of my problems that I have wrestled unsuccessfully with, I offer and give to You. Therefore, I truly feel blessed, O Lord. I feel blessed, sad as I have felt; now I feel glee for I know that You will work everything out and make it all right again. When I bless Thee, O Lord, I also feel truly blessed. Amen."

We brought these affirmations to you so that you could share them with all of mankind, especially for when one feels down upon himself or the world. Tell him to look around and search inside himself until he, too, finds reason to say, *"I feel blessed."*

Have you ever asked yourself the question, "How did I happen to choose this particular time to be born? How was I able to gather enough energy that allowed me to come back to be a teacher (or whatever profession one chose) so as to help mankind?"

The Lord asks, "How indeed did I rescue mankind from all negativity? How did I convince him to change his life around? Was it lessons that I inserted into his mind that stimulated him to understand the value of good living?"

Dear one, if man accepted this thinking, would not all men seek freedom from terror, choosing instead to believe and belong to the Lord? Does this not give life more meaning? Why can we not understand that we can truly reach the top of the mountain if we live closer to the Father?

Then another question was asked: "Even if I disciplined my mind to accept only the most divine and blessed behavior that I promised the Father I would enjoy, will I have to return to the Earth again?" The answer is: "No!" If mankind fully responds to the Father's *Laws* and lives according to the pattern which man himself has consciously chosen, there is no need for him to return to the Earth. He can choose, of course, to come back again to help his fellow man.

We also wish to respond to many questions often asked about what one can expect to find after he passes through the veil. There is no evil man waiting to attack another man on this side of the veil. Thus, no matter how you loved your life on the Earth, you will not receive retribution from another man here. Retribution will only come <u>from you and you alone</u>. You have to judge yourself for the way you have lived.

We would like to conclude with this comment: Each man should live life in the manner that allows him to assemble good energy or light so that when he returns home safely he is rewarded with a good report card!

WHAT SOLOMON TAUGHT

Solomon educated all of mankind by simply living to exemplify his own experiences. He stood for justice and unity among mankind. He did not absolve mankind from their evil thoughts; rather, he simply taught them how to express themselves and to expose their ideals to *Truth*. Then, if mankind still wanted to think in an evil or negative way, Solomon felt that they should have to live alone with their own thinking. He did not hesitate to point out to them that evil thoughts and deeds led to an evil lifetime on the Earth, but that if they would simply obey the Lord's wishes, they could better their lives.

Solomon felt man was obliged to express *Truth*. He felt they owed that part of their life to the Lord Himself, not to anyone else but the Lord. The Lord loves us all equally, he taught; but we owe Him some of our lifetime, too, as repayment for that love. First, we do owe ourselves a life that is simple as well as an honest lifetime while on the Earth; but, the rest of our lifetime we owe to the Father in repayment for His help in guiding and directing our lives while we live on Earth. According to this theory, all of mankind owes the Father the rest of his life. No man owes himself more than he owes the Father.

In the beginning of time, we owed the Lord everything—all parts of our lives—because He directed every portion of a lifetime for us. He sat among us; He taught us how to live a higher life, He directed every move and every thought we had to make, and He exposed us to His *Truths*. He also taught us how to live among mankind down on the Earth. *"You owe your fellowman your heartaches,"* He would often say.

"Why my heartache," we would ask. *"Because,"* the answer came, *"you are obligated to share with each man his heartache; therefore, you owe him your heartache as well."*

Then we would question Him about how it could be possible for all mankind to live down on the Earth together at one time. He said, *"Many of you shall always have to live apart even though I have wanted you always to be together, and some of you will desire to live together. Those of you who cling to one another will exist in peace and harmony. Those of you who strive to live apart will live in disharmony and peace shall elude you forever."* Thus He spelled out for us how He meant for us to live close together to share our celebration of living together with one another as well as our heartaches. He seldom said much more than that, but He often reminded us that as we learned the purpose of our lifetime, He would have more to communicate to us. *"My children,"* He declared, *"learn your purpose while you live on the Earth and be sure to share that also. No man has an idle purpose. It will all amount to something no matter how hard the lesson may be for you to learn. You shall learn it wisely, I hope."* He often repeated that again and again. *"And you shall remain friends throughout all of your lifetime together. You shall gather yourselves together and remain friends. You shall exhaust your entire lives together, but never once shall you speak ill of one another. You have to be compatible with one another. There will be no excuse for hatred or evil thoughts. Thus, My children, thou shall not speak evil of any man. "Therefore, once you learn how to speak only of man's good points, it will come about that only good things will occur in thy lifetime..*

PART IV
DIVINE INTERVENTION
THE LAW OF LOVE

Now to begin a story of *Truth*, I must go back seven years in time to learn how to present these lessons to you so that it makes sense to you and so that you not become annoyed at this repetition of the *Truths* my Masters have brought forth for your education.

Seven years ago I went to my physician for my annual mammogram only to have him inform me that he saw something different on my film. There was a small new growth developing in my left breast. He immediately suggested I go to a surgeon to have a biopsy performed. Shortly after the biopsy report came back it was found to be malignant. At that moment in time, I felt as though a death sentence had just been given to me. Even though I knew that cancer had been a genetic trait in my family— having lost a grandmother, mother and sister from breast cancer—I always felt that I would never have it because I felt I lived too close to God and His Angels that this type of disease surely could not happen to me. My first reaction was total denial, demanding a re-test, but the verdict was the same; yet I still refused to believe this could be happening to me. Then fear and anger were my next emotions. Then I asked the surgeon how soon he could remove this growth and he agreed to do it the next day. Within twenty-four hours I was having my left breast removed.

During the first two nights of post surgery, I felt my Angels around me telling me that I had to experience this, too, so that I could eventually tell those people who came to me for counseling that I knew how they felt—that I, too, had experienced the mastectomy. The second night I heard my Angels say to me that I would survive this, that all of the cancer had been removed, but that I had to make my mind understand and accept this fact and that if I could rein in my fears from having watched my family members suffer and die, I could and would survive.

During the days and nights in the hospital, they kept taking me back and forth from reality of being where I was to the area unknown to many of mankind—it is where the

Angels also go for comfort and I could feel their love and anguish just as I was feeling at that time. They seized upon this occasion to tell me how much God loved me and had He not promised us if we came to Him with a heavy heart we would go away happy and light of heart? I continued to think of that promise and used it like a mantra. Repeating over and over again, I would pronounce to myself, *"I shall return from my visit with the Father with a light heart."* Soon I was discharged from the hospital and sent home.

Each morning upon awakening to a new day, I was so grateful, I never got through thanking God and my blessed Angels. I would get up, go outside and walk the length of our back yard praying all the time for complete healing and saying my mantra. I continued to do that until my husband would call me in for breakfast. After a few weeks of this routine, I began to feel stronger and all the time my teacher would assure me all was well and that I should continue to visit God with my burdens and ask Him to take them away from me. It worked. Soon I began exercising my left arm to strengthen it and get it back over my head. I also started back to my yoga classes. Within a short time, I actually had learned to live without my left breast and not feel uncomfortable about looking at my body. It was then that acceptance had set into being. It was then that I knew I was going to be completely healed. I was most grateful because I did not need further surgery nor did I need any radiation of any kind. My doctor did not feel that I needed to take the medication that prevents further extensions. God had fulfilled His promise to me and that same promise He makes to all of you: *"Come to Me with your burdens and leave with a happy heart."*

Now it is many years from that so-called pronouncement of a death warrant and I have been able to help many women get past that first anger, fear, and acceptance of death. Believe in the Lord. It is that faith that will see you through any situation no matter how difficult.

Having completed this recap about my cancer surgery, the Masters and Teachers were ready to immediately start on more lessons.

MAN SHOULD LOOK INSIDE HIMSELF FOR
THE FATHER'S TEACHINGS

(A Parable)

I am Ishmael. I would like to tell you a story of *Truth*. I have elucidated upon this topic many times and would like to express it here for all of you to hear because it pertains to the healing of a child.

Once there was a small village where simple men lived, but even in their simplicity they never forgot the Father. This particular man that we are going to speak of was one of the most divine men in his village. Every morning upon awakening, his prayers were upon his lips as he greeted the Father with love and blessing even though his own heart was heavy. He had been blessed with two beautiful children whom he had tried to teach. He wanted to teach them all of the blessings that he had been taught as a child, but he finally came to the conclusion that they could not be taught. Somehow, they could not learn. Today, on the Earth, this is termed retardation.

This divine man did not curse the Lord for their condition, but he often wondered what lesson he had to learn so as to enable him to teach these precious retarded children. One particular night as he was praying, he pondered upon this as his heart was anguished saying, "O blessed Father, Thou knowest how much I love Thee and Thou knowest how I live every day of my life and fulfill every *Law* You have prescribed unto me. Why then am I afflicted with not having the knowledge to teach my beloved children? You see me go about Your village teaching all of Your children all of the *Laws* that I have been taught and You know I bring them together to hold services in Your honor. Yet, what have I not learned that I must live with two beautiful children who understand not one word of what I say to them." He began to cry, not in anguish or anger toward the Lord, but for his own inadequacies.

Suddenly, it was as though he was whisked away from his bed. He stood upon the high pathway. Then suddenly before him appeared the Father with the most beautiful bright light shining around Him. The surrounding areas were filled with a mist that was very beautiful to behold, and as he gazed, he cried out, "O Father, is it really You? Am I so blessed as to have You appear to lowly me?" He fell to his knees and began to weep with joy.

The Father said:

"Arise, my son, arise; for you have truly been a great source of joy to Me as I have watched your every action, your every word and your every move. I have seen your anguished heart and I have felt it, and so I say to you now go back among your villagers, go back to your home and continue to teach them as you have in the past and see that they follow the Laws of the Word that has been given; then soon, My son, you will have the blessing that you have prayed and wished upon."

Suddenly the divine man found himself back home, and he immediately went about bringing many of the village children into his home and he began to teach them the *Laws* and *Truths* as had originally been taught to him by the Father. Soon, to his amazement, his own two beautiful children opened their eyes in such a manner that he realized they knew what he had spoken and shortly after they began to speak to him and to each other.

He fell upon his knees and he wept with such great joy for his blessings. He said, "O Holy Father, how can I ever thank You for this wonderful blessing You have brought into my life? You truly see into the hearts of men as well as hear their anguish." He ran into the streets and to each man he met along the way, he said, "You must salute the Lord every day of your life. You must love the Lord with all your heart and all your soul, and you must diligently teach your children to love Him and you must love Him yourself. For it is then that the Holy Father, Who is Master over all of us, will bless you and come into your life."

Among the listeners was one who considered himself even a higher teacher than this divine man, but he felt somehow that the villagers had always given him the short end for he was never assigned duties to teach nor did people come to seek his advice. After having listened to the divine one, he found a way to enter onto the pathway. Then he, too, found himself standing before the Father, but the Father said:

> "You cannot enter here. You must return. You, too, shall be blessed as will all who believe in Me, but you must learn to love men more than you already do. Had you not been a good man, you would not have found the path. Go back now and tell your fellowmen that they are not to try to find this pathway until I call them. When I send for them, they shall then find the pathway back to Me."

So, to this very day, no man enters into the Kingdom with the Father before his time--the time is when the Father calls you back. May God bless you.

KNOWLEDGE IS LIKE A SPRING

The majesty of the Lord's light remains alive within each of our minds. All we need to do is concentrate enough to see the energy spark. It is like a flame in our minds. The wisdom will then roar out, like a newly found spring of water. When a new spring is found, it gushes forth from the Earth with such force that it unearths everything surrounding it. The wisdom flows from man's mind in the same fashion.

Let us now talk about miracles that occur in everyday living. The fact that each man is created with a cleft in his chin in the correct direction is a miracle, but we all expect and accept this miracle from birth. If we accept this as a miracle, then is not our daily living, breathing, etc., not also a miracle?

Living on Earth with God's *Truths* is a required course. The only thing that man volunteers is the time that he takes to learn it. Free will does not mean that you establish the lessons of *Truth*; it means only that you can choose what you want to learn and when you want to learn it.

Love, which is the personification of the Father, cannot be taught per se; however, *Truth* aims to remove the stumbling blocks which blind our awareness to the presence of *love*. *Love* belongs to each man; it is like an inheritance from the Father. What is the opposite of *love*? It is fear. But when love is all encompassing, there is no room for an opposite. In life on Earth, nothing that we call real, as *love*, can be threatened because there is nothing as powerful. Since God's Love--an all-encompassing *love*--dwells within us, why not accept it?

When speaking of miracles, we must also realize that there is no order of progression in difficulties, one is not harder or bigger; they are all the same. All expressions of *love* are of the utmost degree. We must always remember that the source of a miracle is important, not the miracle itself. You see that all miracles mean life and only God is the giver of life. Miracles are natural occurrences. When they do not occur, something has gone wrong in our lives.

The Way to Look Upon Life

When a day is overcast, the world continues to exist and so does mankind. So it is with life. When facing a day full of despair, assert that tomorrow will be brighter. Just as the overcast sky clears, so does life if it is lived correctly with *hope*, *faith*, and *love* in our hearts.

Man should never carry thoughts of revenge. He should try to put himself in the other person's position and see how he would function with that frame of mind. Man never really knows the other man's complete thought. Wisdom comes unto men who think thoughts of *Truth* and who reference all of their thoughts in accordance with the lessons of *Truth* that they have been taught and learned.

WE ARE NEVER ALONE

The Father gave us light so we could live and He also gave us wisdom. He follows us throughout all eternity with His light. We are never alone.

Once, a terrible windstorm came upon us and we were sure we would all be blown away, but He protected us by piling a thin film of His light around us. It was then we felt comfortable, warm, loved, and protected from the winds. We somehow knew then that we would always be protected and watched over, but at the same moment in time we realized that He would never show us His face again while we lived on Earth. Nevertheless, we knew He was always there within our hearts and minds.

THE HONEST MAN

(A Parable)

A young Indian brave learned a lesson about forgetfulness when he stood before the Father, for the Father had to remind him of a deed he had performed long ago which he had deliberately hidden deep within his consciousness so he could forget about it. Once, when he lived in another lifetime before, he stood before the Lord and asked forgiveness for slaying a wild animal. In the past he had killed a wild boar, but he had forgotten about that. What he was now seeking forgiveness for was for killing a wild black bear. He was asking forgiveness for he had sold the skin to others and thus had harvested a gain so he could care for his family.

The Lord spoke with him saying:

"I forgive you this time for slaying the wild animal because your tribe needed food to eat and they had not learned how to harvest the grain which was all about them, but you simply did what you felt you had to do."

Then the Father said to the young brave who stood beside Him:

"Do you not remember that once you slew a boar? How then have you not mentioned that to Me when you asked

to be forgiven?"

In *Truth*, the young brave had forgotten all about killing the boar, but as he looked upon the Father, he asked, "Forgive me again, O Father, for I had truthfully forgotten that incident. It had been so hurtful to me that I had completely wiped it from my memory."

The Lord gazed upon the young brave and responded, with love in His heart saying:

> *"I forgave you long ago for I knew that you needed the food for your tribe and you felt the responsibility to feed all the elders as well as your peers. You did feed them through a hard winter. My son. I forgave you then, and I forgive you now."*

He mused about this for a moment then He said to the guard of the Heavenly Gates,

> *"Set him free. Allow him to roam and feed himself here. You must understand that he is a new man now, starting out anew, so let him get acquainted by setting him free to roam and allow him to refresh himself. Then send him back to Me for I shall honor him by seeing him again. I shall ask him to remain here and live close to Me because he is indeed an honest man and he is worthy of My praise and worthy of praise from all of you who seldom see an honest man coming through these gates safely home to Me. He knows not that I have watched*

him salute Me every morning, no matter how busy he was or how heavy the task of providing for his entire tribe was upon his shoulders. He never forgot Me. He begged Me to forgive him even before he set forth to perform the deed, for it anguished his heart to kill an animal. Yet it was necessary, as this was the only way he saw fit to provide for his tribe. Thus, I forgave him, for do I not live within mankind's heart? Do I not see his wisdom and his illiteracy? Do I not bless him and love him even though he disobeys? Set him free. See to it that he has what he needs as his wants and needs will become a demand in My eyes, so care for him because this mighty brave has returned safely back home, untarnished by present-day standards. Yes, Guard, set him free. Let him roam again and see that his wants and needs are fulfilled with love."

Thus saith the Lord as the young brave advanced further into the garden of the Kingdom of Heaven.

WE EARN OUR JUST DESSERTS

(A Parable)

Here are two simple lessons of *Truth*:

1. We earn our just dessert. If we do something unkind, we will be repaid in kind.

2. We throw caution to the wind. This means we misadvise our minds. When our intuition advises us, we disregard

the advice or warnings.

One day as I was walking along a familiar pathway, I met a man sitting in the middle of the pathway. I heard a familiar, soft-spoken voice saying: *"Do you see that man? He thinks he is the wizard of wisdom."* The voice then asked me if I thought the man looked like a man of wisdom. I hesitated for a moment and then answered, "No, it does not seem possible for him to be so wise because he is sitting where he could be in jeopardy as someone or something could ride over him. Just then a caravan of camels came galloping down this pathway, but the wizard did not move. As soon as the driver saw the man, he stood up thus stopping his caravan of camels for they had been trained to stop immediately when the driver stood up. Then the wise man stood up and began to speak to the master herder; "Please don't go to the top of the mountain as it is full of snow and is dangerous to mount during the nighttime. Why don't you rest your camels and wait for the morning?" The driver would not listen as he was in too big a hurry to reach the top of the mountain so he hurried his caravan of camels on further and faster. No sooner had the wise man sat down again when a second herd of camels came traveling down the road going as fast as the first caravan, but this time the wise man stood up and again advised the driver to slow down and stop to rest. He said, "The sun is dimming and the moonlight will also dim your vision and you might lose your tracking instinct in the dark." But this driver, too, was in a terrible hurry and ignored the warning; thus he proceeded along the pathway at top speed as did the first caravan.

Then suddenly a group of wild animals came along seeking their haven of refuge at the top of the mountain. The wise man stood up in front of the wild animals and he warned them that the two previous caravans of animals and men all had been lost during the night. A thunderous avalanche of snow had buried them. Those who were just stunned drowned the following morning when the sunlight of the day began to melt much of the snow. The snow had not been visible to those men because of their rate of speed and the clarity of the light of the moon was almost nil. He advised the animals to sleep under the trees and bushes near him. He reminded them that tomorrow was another day and they could easily find their pathway leading to their haven of refuge on the mountaintop. They stood for a moment then suddenly their knees bent and then all their haunches went down onto the Earth thus preparing themselves to sleep the night.

Early the next morning they all awakened at one time and were braying for their food. They were distraught and a little distrustful at the nature of this man because he spoke mentally to them in their own language. It suddenly occurred to them that this stranger must be the Lord God Jehovah for had He not indeed saved them from disaster and had He not loved them enough to feed them from His own supply of grain. He did not allow them to travel that first day. He warned them to stay near Him and graze awhile until the sun and snowmelt would have an opportunity to rid the pathway of all the dead carcasses and rid the pathway of any possible disease. He continued to look after them by feeding and watering them until the end of the first day. They then slept another night. He then allowed them to graze another morning. After the second morning He sent them on their way and sure enough He had led them directly to the same pathway which the camels had traveled; only this time, there was no famine and no flood. They found their way safely to the top of the mountain and there they grazed in peace in the hereafter for all eternity.

Mankind is often warned of disasters that come into their lives, but they often disregard these messages brought through dreams and meditation. So it is said, "God provides us all with help." But we disregard it, taking everything at face value and accuse others of disrupting our lives.

Adieu.

DO UNTO OTHERS AS YOU WOULD HAVE
DONE UNTO THEE
(A Parable)

Once upon a time, a man went forth to seek his fortune, when he suddenly found himself surrounded by evil men whom he thought were surely out to rob him. He killed the man closest to him which sent the other three fleeing for their lives. He then confiscated the possessions that they had left behind in their flight for their lives. At that instant, the Lord appeared to him asking:

"Why did you kill that man, that merchant? They were

mercenaries seeking their fortune just the same as you are searching for yours. Why then would you slay one, causing the others to flee for fear of their lives? Do you not know that I, the Lord, love every man just as I love you, equally? Until you have a positive or real reason for that slaying, beware that the remaining men will and can slay you."

Thus saying, the Lord took leave of the man who had slain the mercenary. The traveler began to feel guilty and was overcome with remorse and fear, wondering how he could overcome the stigma of being a murderer for he believed the others would find him and kill him also.

He began to think of God's *Laws* and His *Love*. Thus he sought refuge within those *Laws* by pleading, "I am not able to overcome my distress for my deed. Therefore, I put it into Your hands, God, and I beg Your forgiveness." He then set out once again to seek his fortune, but this time his conscience kept reminding him of his brutal deed. Soon he learned to accuse no man of evil intent, especially not until he had ascertained whether there was any cause for distrust or fear. He continued to mull this over, and he reassured himself that, in the future, he would make sure that the man meant to harm him before he lifted a finger against him. He had learned the *Law* that we never have the right to take another man's life.

After much time had passed, he continued down the original pathway without thinking too much about God's *Laws* or His warning. In his long wandering he had reverted to his old patterns of thinking. As the Father predicted, the three surviving mercenaries crossed his path again; but out of fear, they sought refuge from him for they were sure he would kill them as he had previously done to their friend. The murderer also sought refuge from the three remaining men, hoping they would forgive him by allowing him to live. This standoff came about centuries ago, yet those same three men still search today for the thief who took advantage of them, stealing their fortunes and in turn killing their fellow traveler. Even today, the murderer is still haunted by the same fear that they in turn will kill him.

The original *Law* still remains and the lesson to be learned is *"Do unto others as you would have them do unto thee."*

THE MYNAH BIRD
(A Parable)

The Lord came back into our lives to illuminate our thinking process in order to help us in our time of need. He places His wonderful *Laws* and teachings into our minds. He explains them in depth to us and relates what He wishes us to do with them; that is: to remember them and teach them to His other children.

Now, for the parable which we recount for you from your meditation. There seems to have been a time on the Earth when the Father sought to control men's minds, but it was a futile attempt on His part because mankind seemed to liken His teachings and healings to an adverse situation instead of welcoming Him by trying to learn. It was as though they were hiding their heads in the sand from Him. They would not listen and did not care to learn about the healing of their own minds or their own bodies. As always, there were those who would take advantage of their fellowman. Evil men strode upon the Earth during that period of time trying to teach the others their negative ways and thoughts. Soon, the Father was desperate in

His attempt to save the men that He had placed upon the Earth from those evil influences. He set about to correct this situation. First, He taught some of His very finest Masters and Teachers all the *Original Truths*. Again and again He went over the original lessons and *Laws* and He sent them to the Earth.

Very soon after they became acquainted with their fellowman, these teachers became selfish and did not want to share the original lessons. They felt that if they did not share the lessons, they would live closer to the Lord without any competitors, that they alone would hold all the knowledge when they returned. They believed the Lord would never know what they were doing and so they, too, hid their heads in the sand, so to speak. They felt they had learned the *Truth* the hard way and did not want to just dispense these *Truths* among all those they met. They thought it was too easy; it was like feeding them with the silver spoon. So they started to teach evil thoughts to mankind, twisting the Lord's lessons and *Laws* saying that the Lord had sent them to institute these new teachings.

Soon, the Lord heard the anguished cries issuing from the hearts of the men He had placed upon the Earth. The new

Teachers began gnashing their teeth in disappointment when they saw the men would not listen to them either. The Teachers became frightened with these events and they too sought refuge from the Lord. Alas, they knew the *Truth*, the Lord must know this and would never forgive them for substituting their thoughts for His *Truths* and thus placing negativity into the minds of His children. Their teaching had changed the meaning of *Truth Everlasting* (all *laws*, all *truths*) so completely that even the Lord could not understand it. But He forgave them, as He always forgives His children. As He stood before them, He offered them a choice:

> *"You can either remain upon the Earth and teach the Original lessons that I have taught you or abdicate your authority as Teachers and come back home and re-learn your lessons."*

Of course, these very selfish and stiff-necked Masters did not want to return. So they sought refuge from the Lord and remained alive on Earth. The Lord gave this decision considerable thought and decided to send His favorite mynah bird but first He reviewed all the *lessons* before He sent the bird to the Earth. The Lord advised the bird to whisper His messages into mankind's mind. The mynah bird did indeed visit Earth, and he soon flew among mankind and began whispering the *first lesson*. Then he said, "I shall return very soon with the *second lesson*, but you must remember the words exactly as I have spoken them unto thee."

Soon the Lord felt that the mynah bird had been given enough time to teach His children the *first lesson* and He began to seek after the bird in order to review the bird's mind. He wanted to retrain him for the *second lesson*, but to His horror He found that the very men to whom the mynah bird had taught the *first lesson* and to whom he had promised to return with the *second lesson* had slaughtered the mynah bird so that he could not teach the *lessons* to anyone else. The Lord said, *"You now see the lessons have ended and I shall seek refuge from you."*

He did not send any punishment to the wicked men because He is a benevolent Father and He wished them well, but He called them together and said to them:

> *"Because you have been selfish and have slaughtered My precious mynah bird, because of your selfishness, you have wasted this your lifetime on Earth. As long as you live on Earth in this lifetime you shall never learn a*

single solitary thing. When you return again to live on Earth, you shall have to relearn every thought I have ever taught thee, and you shall have to live on the Earth as many times as necessary until you relearn every word of the Original Laws which I have taught you."

He then vanished from sight. The wise men of that time understood their punishment. They would have to live alone without the Father's help for as long as they dwelled on the Earth. Then they recalled the saying:

"The Lord knows every sparrow that He puts down upon the Earth, and if you destroy one of His sparrows, you might just as well have destroyed one of His children. You have destroyed a part of Him."

And the wise men wept.

WHEN THE STUDENT IS READY, THE MASTER APPEARS

(A Parable)

Dear child, before we begin to tell you the parable that we spoke to you about last night, we would like to clear up a fact for man because it is something that is often asked: "Why does my Master not appear to me?" We want all to know that any man can have an audience with his Masters and Teachers if he becomes a true mediator--true unto himself as well as his

Teachers--unless his mind is clogged with negative thoughts. So many students have so little faith in themselves and make such comments as, "I cannot do this. There is something wrong with me. I am not worthy of a Teacher," etc. All of this negativity clogs the mind so that relaxation cannot come about; therefore, poor results do. If the student is sincere and will practice clearing his mind before sitting down for his meditation, very soon, he will find peace of mind, relaxation, joy and illumination.

The Parable of the Prized Student

And now, to commence with the parable: Once upon a time there was a brilliant student and all of the Masters and Teachers wanted to be his teacher. So the highest of Teachers came into the student's mind and began to expand upon various subjects. At first the student listened intently, no matter what or how long the speeches were. He was the greatest student. One day the Master Teacher noticed his student's mind was wandering back and forth over less important things. This continued for some time. The Master Teacher then began to realize he was wasting his time, and so he no longer appeared to that student.

Soon after his departure, a second Teacher appeared and he began to teach this student about *Truth Everlasting*. Almost at once he began to sense that the student had been more adequately trained by the first Teacher; and the teacher doubted his own ability to teach this student but continued anyway. The student became despondent; realizing that he was not being taught the whole *Truth*, the student began to regret that he had not listened more attentively to the first Master Teacher. He began to search for his first Teacher and he kept saying to himself, "If I only could find my first Teacher, I would first apologize for not listening and I would promise him to never again close my mind to him, no matter how long his dissertations would become."

The second Teacher, sensing that his student was no longer interested in his type of teaching, promised that he would try to locate the first Teacher. Of course, the second Teacher was not sincere for he really wanted to be able to teach this prized student. Because of his insincerity, he made very few inquiries into the whereabouts of the original Teacher.

Then one night a vision occurred to the student and he saw

where he could find his first Teacher. This first Teacher's message to the student was, "All you ever have to do is call out to me. Had you only done that, I would have appeared long ago." Upon awakening, the student sat down and earnestly prayed that his first Teacher would come back to him, and so it happened. The response came about immediately, but his Teacher's warning was "If you do not listen attentively enough, I shall disappear forever."

And so, unto this very day, that student and that Teacher are united in purpose, seeking happiness and peace for the entire universe of mankind.

ALTERED CONSCIOUSNESS

Today is another beautiful day, and we are happy to greet you. Mankind little realizes what a part God plays in his life everyday, which is very sad as far as we are concerned. If each man were more intimate with God, he would enjoy his life much more and life would have so much more meaning that he would automatically want to fulfill that which he came to do.

We wonder if you have paid much attention to the altered state of consciousness--the state of mind which both allows you to receive information and for us to be able to deliver it to you. You see, the state of consciousness allows your mind to operate on the same vibratory rate as ours—allowing us to speak and you to hear us. Just as in electricity if the plug is of a different current from your appliance, it doesn't work. This phenomenon depends upon our universal training and the knowledge we have brought back with us.

Mankind does not understand that this process takes place all the time--when you sleep as well as when you meditate. We learn what is within your mind; thus, you are re-educating us as well as our helping you. In accordance with that line of thinking, we want to help you at this particular moment since you are asking us about *Truth Everlasting.* You see, with us it is a constant vigilance to watch over those to whom we have been assigned, so to speak, both while they sleep and while they are awake. Few think about this while we live down on the Earth. We obviously are too unaware of what is truly happening to us while we live on the Earth. We are so wrapped up in our daily little lives trying to accomplish what we feel we must materially accomplish, that we do not think of the overall picture. The overall picture is about *Life Everlasting* that is a continuation of life going on forever and ever. Our short life that we now live on the Earth is just like a dot in the universe. It is as you might even say like a "star in the vast heavens." It is very, very minute.

After we are taken or removed from the environment of the Earth, we feel a great deal of remorse that we did not understand the value of life or that we did not do our utmost to accomplish what we really had the ability to accomplish while on the Earth even though we had promised to do so. When you stop to think about it, who stands to lose more than we do if we do not envision our own greatness while we live down on Earth?

Just think: You were really able to learn how to alter your consciousness and alter your thinking because your mind is like a computer. You can learn. You can change. When we realize these things and we make the most of our lives, then we have nothing to regret when our time upon the Earth is over. You see, occasionally we must remember that the Father dispenses *Truth* into our minds. I say <u>occasionally</u>, but the cause for that is that we only occasionally allow ourselves to hear the *Truth*

He dispenses. Yes, He does dispense *Truth* and we must learn to listen more intently.

In addition to the daily guidance and recommendations the Father brings to us, He also brings us daily lessons of *Truth* with which, if we would just follow His advice, and if we listen more carefully to His teaching on a daily basis, He will teach us how to excel in all walks of life while we are living on the Earth.

He offers His advice early each morning just before we awaken, when He brings our daily light. When we sleep during the night, He advises us how to speak and act in a proper manner; but He also advises us how to resist all sorts of temptation which could lead us astray. So if we listened to our alter egos, the Father could be actively alive along side us on a daily basis, just exactly as we are doing today as we have this discourse with you. He expects us to listen exactly in the same manner, only He inculcates His thoughts into our minds early each morning to provide us with the necessary information, knowledge and charm (yes, charm) that we need to succeed. He also advises us in the manner which will make our lives successful, thus fulfilling our original plan. He never forgets our original covenant; thus, He tries to guide us to help fulfill them. He also devises the manner that makes our lives successful. If He felt a million dollars would be the answer to sweeten our lives and make our lives successful, He would bestow the knowledge into our minds so that this could also happen.

Believe us when we tell you this is the truth. Why people strive so much and so hard for material values that have no meaning on this side is beyond us. It would seem that over generations of living, mankind would have learned that the only things that have true worth or meaning are the spiritual things. The knowledge that you learn about yourself, about mankind and about how you might help mankind is what you are expected to bring home with you. You do not return with one material thing.

The Father devises many means for us to accomplish our goals. Our attention is drawn away from the millions or materialism that we spoke about allowing us to fulfill our lives in another manner. To assert His will upon our minds, the Father provides us with what we need to be successful. If that does not please us and we desire to be even more successful, we must then ask for His directions and ask how to make our lives more successful than we think they are at the present time. He sends Master Teachers into your lives every day to help you to be more successful in planning your near future. He wants each man to use the talents with which he came to Earth. He begs mankind to learn the true value of living on the Earth. It is so much easier to learn and accomplish these things while you are on the Earth than when you return as a spirit. The Father will send to you only that which you need to make your life meaningful.

Now allow us to take leave of you, my child. We hope that the discourse, which we brought to you this day, will help to simplify some of the thoughts that we find racing through your minds. Yes, man can complete in a second that which would take him a year on this side if he would only use that second wisely while he lives on Earth. Yes, God is a constant guide and companion to all of man. Yes, God sends to us the Masters and Teachers that we need to help us realign our minds to combine all the ideas and thoughts that we came back to live with so that we can fulfill the promise we made to Him so many centuries ago. And yes, the Holy Father blesses each and every man for He loves them all equally.

Let us leave you with this prayer:

"Help us, O Lord, to find the happiness and joy we need to feel in this lifetime; help us to understand fully the life in which we now live; help us to learn how to comfort the poor, the lame of the body, of the heart, of the spirit and of the soul." Amen.

THE HEAVENLY ABODE OF OUR MIND

We know some may find the repetition of what the Father tries to teach mankind endless, but this is the only way we know to impress man's mind. For a long time, He has asked us to ascend to His *Heavenly Abode*. What we mean to say is that man should bring his level of thinking up to the level of consciousness that enables him to understand the Father's thinking. Thus, my child, if man would only understand if he followed the Father's directions, he could overcome negativity or anything untoward that could happen in this lifetime. He trains our minds to ascend to that *Heavenly Abode*—that haven of refuge, that area within our own minds that every man has.

What we are trying to say so that man can understand is that every man has in his mind an area that we refer to as the *"Heavenly Abode"* or the *"Kingdom of Heaven."* Even as we speak today, there are those in terrible need of understanding how high is up, how deep is down, and how far is out. Man should understand that these concepts are referring to his mentality and consciousness. If only man would allow himself the opportunity to ascend and extend himself into His *Heavenly Abode*, he could amass enough wisdom and knowledge to help him set his life straight throughout his life while living on the Earth.

We your Master Teachers, try to study man's mind. This allows us to see how deeply etched are his plans or purpose in life. We speak of this in these terms so that man will understand that the plan of life is deeply etched into his consciousness and is referred to as the "yellow brick road."

We have taught men to explore the unknown universe by way of their fantasies. Fantasy allows our minds to lift toward attaining the high heavenly glory of thought. Einstein would take time during the day to go to Central Park to rest his mind, to meditate. After a short time, he felt his mind was cleared and answers came more easily. Man's preconceived notions can also deter him from succeeding within his lifetime. *We are trying to help man fulfill what he came to do.* Therefore, we try to rid his mind of the negative forces that could deter him from succeeding. We are not allowed to live a man's life because each person is given his own free will, but we try desperately hard to point out the negativity so that man can inculcate these positive thoughts for there are certain men whose negativity is so deeply seated that they rebuff our attempts to guide them.

The road map of men's lives is determined before their birth, and we are not allowed to change that. We are not allowed to go too far into the future plans that they have designed for themselves utilizing their *free will.* Our purpose of extracting his negativity is to help man rid himself of the *negative roadblocks* placed into his mind by *himself.* There is an equal opportunity for all of mankind either to hide his head in shame for his lost opportunities or elevate his head in glory. It is his choice. *Free will* dictates what is happening down on the Earth during this lifetime.

We advise man to lift up his head and set his course free of involvements that would deter his growth. We say, "Set your course higher than usual; set your thermometer on high so that your meter of thinking can accelerate your temperature and allow your mind to expand in consciousness. Remember, my child, your *consciousness* is *equal* to your *thinking*. If you evolve to a higher rate of thinking, evolutions or thoughts occur, and you will begin to understand every single signal transmitted into your mind so that you will begin to follow the right pathway and grow in consciousness."

In the morning as man arises from his bed, he should try to set his mind free, thank the Lord for the new day, ask for guidance and directions, and listen carefully to every syllable that is uttered to him. If man practices this everyday, eventually he will understand what the Father wishes for him for that day.

In closing, we wish to make this assertion: It would take divine intervention alone to lead man out of the predicament in which he now finds himself if he does not bring the Lord back into his life. That is man's predicament because he has forgotten how to communicate with the Father. We from this side ask how long will it take man to extend his hand to the Lord and ask--and yes beg--to be taught the *Original Laws* again.

EVICT NEGATIVITY FROM YOUR MIND
AS MAN THINKS, SO HE IS

Man is constantly being taught, *"Truth—Almighty Truth."* Negativity does not linger long in mankind's heart or mind <u>unless</u> he allows it to live there. The ancient laws that were taught us centuries ago taught us of an incident that occurred within one man's lifetime. This particular man was constantly exposed to negativity, but he refused to accept it. He would evict the negativity each time it was placed into his mind. He never allowed it to live there long enough to attach itself to his heart or soul, nor did he allow it time to feel at home within him. He used this ancient prayer:

> *"Come back into my life, O merciful Father, and take this evil thought out of my mind. Do not allow it to attach itself unto me for I fear if evil involved me further into its grasp, I might remain alive forever on this Earth without fulfilling my mission. Please take away the hurt and the heartache that I might feel peace. And please, Father, rejoice with me that I understand how to dispose of this*

evil and the woebegotten thoughts. Unlike other men, I rejoice in You, Father, and I gather my energy each morning through Your light. This I know and I rejoice within my heart and soul knowing full well that You are the Almighty Father over all of mankind and that You would not release unfit or misspent energy into my mind. Amen."

This is the message of *truth* we came to teach you today. Even as men sit down to their dinners tonight, do they ever look upon the Lord as their friend, as their benefactor? No. They disdain His name and live aimlessly alone along this life's pathway. They hope someday to change their lives. Well, procrastinator, now is the time for change! Stop harboring negative thoughts and allowing them to root into your consciousness for it then becomes more difficult to cleanse them from your mind.

Our advice to those who desire to live the *Universal Laws* is to live them moment by moment, day by day, allowing the Messengers and Teachers the freedom to place the positive thoughts into their minds while at the same time expelling all negative thinking. The Lord loves us all. He wants only good for His children. Instant success can come to the man who beholds the Lord's light and love and lives within His messages of *Everlasting Truth*. Allow us to leave you with this prayer:

"Allow us the freedom, O Lord, to live in Your sunlight which You and You alone possess. Give to us the understanding to separate Truth from evil, to sort out the fiction from the fact and allow us Your love by giving us the privilege of knowing Your love even more intimately and intently. O Father, give to us the illumination we need to understand Thy words. Father of Mercy, allow us happiness and joy. Allow us the education we need to survive during this lifetime. Help us by renewing our energy daily and giving to us the strength of character that we need to succeed in this lifetime. Amen."

HE SHUTTERS OUR MINDS FROM EVIL

The Father wanted us to question our lives. He taught us to think profound thoughts such as the following: Why did I choose this time to be born? Why did I come back here to be educated? Why did the Father come back to teach us again and again? Am I truly fulfilling my purpose on the Earth?

The Father wonders why simple-minded men living today can hold agnostic views. Where is the wisdom the Father had taught us? Why is it so deeply buried that we cannot account for it at all? As an example, if man buried himself in filth, would he not have simply tried to wash the filth off himself or would he have continued to wear it, showing mankind that he did not know how to wash himself and be free of filth? That is the question that the Father often asks us.

Therein is a simple solution to our plight, which is: wash out your mind; let all negativity go. Stop fantasizing and try to find the deeper meaning of *Life Everlasting*. We who are your *Messengers of Truth* ask ourselves who had dictated these words to us that cause us to stand along side of you today? What is necessary and expected of us to teach and to think? Who is responsible? Who is the prime mover over every facet of our lives? The answer again is a simple one. It is our beloved and most benevolent Father who stands along side of each and every one of us. Why He does not decline the questionable honor of working with us today we cannot understand, for the wisdom that He has taught us has disappeared from the Earth. Seldom does the Father hear a man or woman utter a real *Truth* today. Today they commune with one thought, *"Thou shalt not commit adultery,"* yet they do not even live that one *Law*. Who condemns them? *"Not I,"* says the Father, *"I condemn no man.*

I regulate his life only in that I supply his energy. Did I not give man free will?"

These are the thoughts we feel must go through His mind when He looks down upon the Earth. These thoughts are only an educated guess. We ask ourselves again, "Why can't man enjoy a simple life with happiness and contentment, peace and harmony, while he is down on Earth?" All man needs to do is obey the *Original Commandments*. Who among us lives by the Lord's *Commandments* as they were originally taught to us? Who among us dares to say that we live by <u>every</u> *Commandment* that has been taught to us? Little is known about the many more commandments which had originally been given to Moses because Moses put them aside for fear he could not control the heathen pack of men with even the original ten. They so fumed and fussed with him when he returned with the original ten *Commandments* that at times he almost gave up hope of ever teaching them to live God's *Laws*.

When man allows himself to think along these lines, his education becomes wisdom, and the images of himself as well as of the Father becomes more clearly pronounced, and then he truly begins to understand that there is a Living God who cares about all of mankind.

God taught us to allow our minds to wander far and wide and to accept the energy that we receive by using our minds in this fashion; He even condoned our fantasies for He wanted us to remember that once we had stood upon the mountain top close to Him and that He taught us how to mentally send out messages to all men. He taught us to give hope to man to help him to find purpose. That would be more easily done if man lived each day close to the Father. The Lord taught us that without love and hope, life could not continue. Leave man with *Hope*.

Without hope, man suffers irreparable depression and loss of purpose. Incomparable happiness and joy come from hope. If he just would sit down and think about life, he could easily understand how hard life could be without hope. He would know that his on-going education would suffer and that he would be limiting himself in this life. Thus, life would feel hopeless to him. The reason that his education would suffer is that man would fear extending his mind beyond familiar horizons—thus establishing limitations upon himself. Can you not see that the Father's wisdom eliminates the negative sources of trouble from man's mind, that wisdom makes it possible for man to reason negativity away and not suffer pangs of fear? The man who looks upon himself as insignificant, while living down on the Earth today is fearful of life and often wonders why he is even living. His heraldic angels try to tell him, "Calm your heart, calm your soul, accept life and live with hope in your heart, not despair."

Through prayer and meditation man can establish contact with his higher self. The quotation, "Suffer the little children to come unto Me" means help yourself, help others—do not allow yourself to suffer indefinitely. Set yourselves free. Set yourselves free, my children. Set yourselves free!

After man learns to free himself from fear, he can then climb the steps of the ladder alone without the help of available Teachers. He can say to them, "Come and stand along side me and see how strong I have become without your assistance, but just be there in case I should ever need you again."

For, one solitary moment, see yourself and allow yourself to see immortality, alone, without fear. Free yourself from the fear that haunts men's souls. Say to any man who would hurt you or doubt you, *"I see the Lord. He is ever standing along side of me. He will not allow me to slip back into the situation where I would have to live in fear. Can't you embrace Him also?"*

The Father continues to caution us to live on high. He loves and cares for us as He does for all of His children. We promised long ago that no other God would be worshipped other than He. He is part of the universe of which we, too, are a part. He needs all of mankind to help Him spread these words of wisdom so that He does not have to live alone because, unfortunately, few men who live today truly believe in a Living God. They do not believe or understand that He has taken a direct part in their present life as He has during all their lifetimes before.

The Father has shuttered our minds from evil or negative intent. He has helped us over the threshold of evil into the *Land of Truth*. If only we would relentlessly seek after Him! He continues to teach us by the events that happen to us each day on our pathway.

OUR COVENANT

The Father comes back into our lives each morning as we have often said. When mankind becomes aware of the opportunities that he has missed by not accepting the Father, he will feel remorse, especially at the time when he passes over to the other side of the veil. He will regret not having expanded his consciousness when the opportunity had presented itself. No matter how long it takes us to learn to accept the Father as our partner in our daily lives, He continues to love us and willingly teaches us when we do finally awaken to the necessity of knowing His *Laws.*

In the beginning, He ordered us to remain vital; and after a certain length of time, He had hoped that we would reiterate our vows, so to speak, for we made many promises to Him before re-entering the Earth. The one promise <u>all</u> of mankind made was to reach out, to teach and communicate with others. Unfortunately, man has forgotten the promise and the vows that he had taken. Today, heresy is being taught on the Earth instead of *Truth.*

Since we are given *free will,* many will deliberately forget about our vows and wander around as free spirits and souls, so to speak; but when the Lord remands us back home and when we stand beside Him, man then remembers all that he had wished to be and how far he remains from having completed his journey on the Earth.

It is then up to us as to how we are going to fulfill our mission, for in truth, we <u>will</u> fulfill that mission. He, being the Loving Father that He is, stimulates our mind again and again and sets our souls free to wander and roam. He continues to do this until we finish what we originally promised to do. He views us as willful children and so He demands that we remain with Him until we learn to expand our consciousness to the heights that He expects of us. Then again, He reins us back in, so to speak, and teaches us again not to be willful, but to understand how hard it is to control millions of souls each day. He would appreciate if we would cooperate with Him and start each morning anew. He despairs at our inadequacies just as Earthly parents do when they watch their children go astray, for He is indeed a most loving parent. He knows that if we would live closer to Him and listen to His guidance, we could accomplish what we originally set out to do.

The Father renounces racism and such other complexities of hatred that have cropped up in society today for He did not teach His children hatred. The Father today considers what His alternatives might be. Being a loving Father, He finds it difficult to contemplate extermination of all His children. This will indeed become a reality if mankind does not change their way of living although perhaps not in this generation of people.

Thus, my children, the wise man treats the Father with respect each morning, wishes Him well and issues thoughts of love for Him. As for man, the Father continues to educate him each morning so that he might survive among his fellow men. He is able to weigh exactly how much energy each man needs each day to perform his duties. Thus, if man has a difficult day caused by stress, etc., he might feel short-changed of energy and take to bed early.

He allows us freedom to explore the universe each night as we sleep. He allows our souls to travel out into the universe seeing other galaxies, visiting with other peoples—men, women and children—who are just like us. But additional education is needed for that precept of thinking, and we can only go so far because the energy is limited and thus the Father teaches us wisely to remain alive within our galaxy. He sends us forth, only at night, to teach each other lessons of *Truth Everlasting*. We have an exchange of energy or knowledge from them. You might be interested in this bit of knowledge: The galaxies are a formidable source. Little is known as to how the Earth was set free to bounce back upon its axis alone.

We want to end with this prayer. Lift up your face on a daily basis and say unto Him:

> *"Beloved Father, come into my life, seek me out and help me to find the happiness and joy that You promised me from the very beginning of time. And please, O Heavenly Father, take away all negative thoughts, replacing them with Truth, happiness and joy.*

> *Amen."*

EPILOGUE
ANGELGRAPHS

The angelgraphs on the front and back covers of this book were taken by Marcie Taylor from her home near Girard, KS. Marcie is a kindergarten teacher who lives on a farm with her husband Mark and two sons. On July 10, 1997, as she was looking out the west window of her living room watching her mother-in-law drive out of the yard with her two sons, she saw her angel in the clouds. She grabbed her camera and ran outside. The angel was quite large and completely filled the viewfinder of her camera. She took two pictures using the zoom lens and one picture showing the relationship of the angel to trees in the foreground. Marcie says the angel hovered in the sky for about 20 minutes.

Driving to Wal-Mart to pick up the pictures, she said a little prayer that the pictures would be as vivid as she recalled but ended the prayer with, "Thy will be done." She had ordered 5 x 7 prints and when she saw the three breathtaking pictures, she started trembling. Standing next to her was Dr. Kenneth Bryant, Girard chiropractor, who was rather startled when Marcie started pounding on his arm with tears in her eyes. When he saw the pictures, he too was overcome with emotion.

When she got home with her precious pictures, her 11-year-old son, Matthew, told her he had also seen the angel from his grandmother's car and had told her and his younger brother, Myles, about it. The senior Mrs. Taylor confirms his story.

Marcie was diagnosed with multiple sclerosis in 1993 when she was 29 years old. Since the visit with her angel a year ago, her MS has gone into remission through new medication and an abiding faith in God. She feels that the angel was sent to her by God as a message to her that she was going to be all right and to spread the news of His existence.

She made a promise to herself to distribute pictures of the angel to 1,000 people. She has paid for all the reprints herself and refuses payment of any kind and has already shared her angel with over 1,100 people. Marcie is pleased that pictures of the angel have been sent all over the world.

At this same time, Bess, the author of this book, was struggling with ideas for the cover of her new book. A friend of Bess "just happened" to come in contact with Marcie and showed a copy of the photo to Bess. She immediately knew that this should be on the cover and that, as always, God had blessed her with that which she needed.

Marcie agreed because the book is sold as a non-profit item as is all of Bess' material.

Oh yes, The camera that took the angelgraphs hasn't worked since.

MORE SPIRITUAL TRUTHS AVAILABLE
FROM PESHA PUBLISHING

#1.. Bess's other book *How To Find Your Way Back Home.* Price..$16.95 + $3 for shipping and handling...Total- $19.95.

#2.. Additional copies of *Heaven On Earth Is A Mission*-$16.95 plus $3 for shipping and handling...Total-$19.95

#3..*THE MASTERS SERIES* (PART #1)..............................

A six audio cassette program recorded in Bess's own voice.

Tape #1...FEAR...........................Tape #2...PURPOSE

Tape #3...HAPPINESS..................Tape #4...HOW TO FACE LIFE

Tape#5...SEVEN STEPS TO PERFECTION.....Tape #6...HEALING

You may purchase the tapes singly at $12 each + $2 for S&H...total $14 ea. Or for the best value you may purchase all six as a set for $55. When you purchase as a set you save $17.00 on the cassettes and we will pay all your shipping and handling charges. Your savings is $29.00. To order send a check or money order to:

PESHA PUBLISHING--**P.O. BOX 47484--PHOENIX, ARIZONA 85068-7484. Please include your complete (PRINTED) shipping address and a description of the product you are ordering.**